PREFACE

HOW IT ALL STARTED...

" Jean Christophe Boele van Hensbroek, the publisher of my books, phoned me: 'Would you like to make a book about Amsterdam?'

'No,' I said. 'I won't do that because then I would have to draw everybody's back garden and that is not possible. People will look to see whether their garden is in the book and, if it is, they'll buy it. If it's not in there, they'll think, "What an awful book." So, no.'

And then I thought that Amsterdam is not a good idea, but Holland is a really nice idea. Everybody understands that I can never really copy the entire country precisely so I am free to combine things that would never really appear together.

I started sketching my ideas. I thought that would not take me too long.

When the sketches were ready, I went to the publisher to ask him whether he liked them, but he made a face and remarked: 'They are pretty busy...'

'Charming!' I exclaimed. 'I've got to squeeze a whole country into just twelve illustrations!'

'Yes, but the dunes are missing...'

'Yes? Hello? Where? Where should I put them?'

'Make twice as many pages,' he finally conceded.

I was really happy with that, but it wasn't until I got home that I realized that this also meant twice as much work. In the end, it took me three years.

First, I had to scout the country. I also had a wonderful old atlas, which I read from cover to cover.

I started with the ground. What is Holland made of? I knew nothing about that at all, and if I made up something myself, there was bound to be some angry people and you don't want that. If I was going to draw something, I wanted to see it with my own eyes. So, I set out on my travels and I became more and more fanatical.

I wrote down everything that came into my head, but that became such a total mess that I couldn't figure it out. So then I made an alphabet. After the 'A' I wrote: Amsterdam, Asparagus, ANWB, the kid's track of Assen (after all, it is a children's book). After the 'B' I wrote down Biesbosch, Bridges, Beschuit...

Then, I started asking the people around me. At first, the Dutch grumble a bit, but then they say: 'Yes, and you really must put this in, it's very important!' So then I wrote down after the 'F' Fierljeppen and after the 'G' Graffiti—because writing on the walls everywhere is also typically Dutch.

Slowly but surely, order gradually took over from chaos. Next I thought that every page should contain a Dutch nursery rhyme and something from Dutch children's literature as homage to my comrades. And, while I was at it, I would also put a bit of history onto each page. The canon of Dutch History has fifty topics and I had room for all fifty. [These topics are marked with an C in this book.]

Some illustrations also contain paintings. I often go to look at paintings and I wanted to give the children who looked at this book a bit of a treat. It doesn't matter if you don't see the references to the paintings. If you do, then you can have some fun. And if you see a detail of a painting pass by, it may stay in your mind and when you one day visit the museum you can say to yourself, 'Hey, I've seen that before.'

If that happens, I'm satisfied."

THE DUTCH

"Making this book has made me like the Dutch people more and more. If I'm in France, I recognize Dutch visitors from a mile away: windbreakers, sensible shoes, good bikes, and riding into the wind. At midday, they eat sandwiches from a plastic bag. They are easily annoyed and quick to criticize— that's what I like least. The Dutch like sailing, preferably into the wind, with no nonsense.

The Dutch love symmetry. Just take a look at a Dutch bay window: the curtains are identically pleated on both sides—they actually measure them!— with a plant in the middle. There may also be two plants, but then they must grow so that they mirror each other. The orchid, for example, is 'in,' and if there are two orchids they have to be exact mirrors of each other. If they are not identical, it's just not as good. There should also be two wooden ducks next to them.

What I find so special about the Dutch—and I really mean this!—is that they are so simple in their friendship. You can turn up with a hole in your sweater and you'll still be welcome. This really is true—you can get close to Dutch people because they don't keep you at a distance. You are really welcome and they even invite you to stay with them. However, they don't like it if you arrive at six in the evening because that's when they eat. I soon found that out. People in France would say at such an occasion: 'Sit down, and I'll get you something to drink!', but the Dutch won't say anything...

Unsuspecting, I would arrive at six o'clock when I hadn't lived in Holland for long. I had no idea that they would be at the table and that they really don't want to you pull up a chair, because there's not enough food. That's Dutch. Yet, I've found the finest friends in the world here. I would never change them.

And, of course, there's Sinterklaas. That feast is such fun. Sinterklaas is gold and looks fantastic. His helpers, the Piets, are rascals and there are great traditional songs that people still sing at the top of their voices. They've thought up all sorts of delicacies for the festival, and each year they are made with the same commitment. It is a great party for small persons and for grownups. I know some people who write complete literary poems for Sinterklaas Evening. Others celebrate by putting together wonderful surprises. Where else do you have something like that? Nowhere. Only here. "

HOLLAND

THE RECURRING ELEMENTS

"If you say to a child: 'Come and look at this', then he'll look and say: 'Seen it.' But if you persist: 'But did you see this? And that?,' then the child will really look and you'll have his attention. That's why I wanted a number of recurring elements in every illustration in order to sharpen the focus of children so they will recognize things that don't move around, that stay in Holland, and are really Dutch."

"I liked the yellow balloon because I made a book about a yellow balloon in the past. And it's quick to draw, and that's good too."
The yellow balloon by Charlotte Dematons first appeared in 2003.

"The heron is a real Dutch bird that doesn't move around. It stays here for the winter."

"A gnome has nothing to do with Holland, except that you often see him standing in the garden. For the fun of it, I made this little gnome who appears on every spread."

"A friend of ours, who has since retired, has a bus from the 1970s. While I was working on this book, he toured around Holland and sent me mail: 'Did you know that this or that...?' Then I thought: 'Geert-Jan must appear in the book with his bus.'"

"Paul Biegel is one of my favorite authors, so the sea-worthy little boat the Never-sink that belongs to the Little Captain is included as homage to him."
The Little Captain was written by Paul Biegel (1925-2006) and illustrated by Carl Hollander (1934-1995). It appeared for the first time in 1970.

"Here we have the Chameleon, the boat belonging to the twins Hielke and Sietse from the classic children's book. They can really sail it along all the inland waters in Holland."
The first part of the series about Sietse and Hielke by author Hotze de Roos (1909-1991) appeared in 1949, was entitled The Skippers of the Chameleon, illustrated by Pol Dom (1885-1970). De Roos wrote a total of sixty volumes, most of which were illustrated by Gerard van Straaten (1924-2011), who drew the well-known picture of the twins. Since the death of Hotze de Roos, several new stories have appeared about Sietse and Hielke written by other authors.

"Finally there is Black Piet. For my own amusement, I let this Piet miss the boat in December. He didn't really know his geography very well, so it is difficult for him to find the way back to Spain but he does finally succeed."
Black Piet is the helper of Sinterklaas. He listens to whether children are singing songs or are naughty, and climbs down the chimney to put their presents in their shoes. He is as "black as soot" from climbing down the chimneys. He always wears a page's suit, a large white collar, and a cap with a feather.

"When I started the book, I came up against a problem in that Holland is actually made up of only two colors: green and blue. The green of the grass, of the trees, the nature and the blue of the water, the canals, the lakes, the rivers, the sea, etc. I wanted a greater variety in color and so I decided to alternate the seasons. However, that wasn't enough because the sea remains more or less the same. Then suddenly it came to me that I could show both day and night. If I could play with that, it would give me different types of color. I could look forward to Amsterdam by night and that is really beautiful! The next question soon arose: where does Holland begin? There's really no start.

We all know that Holland is made of tulips, clogs, and windmills. Something that is even more present is water. The Dutch are always doing something with water. They swim in it, sail on it, and, if it suddenly freezes, they go crazy and they all want to skate on the ice. So I decided to start with the water, on the sea. The Dutch journeyed to the East and were on the sea all the time, and I wanted to show that—the far-off sea, at night."*

NIGHT
THE FAR-OFF SEA

THE VOC AND PEPPER NUTS

C **DE VERENIGDE OOSTINDISCHE COMPAGNIE**
(VOC—United East Indies Company, 1602-1799)

OVERSEAS EXPANSION
Since Spain had forbidden the Republic of the United Netherlands to trade with Spain and Portugal, various Dutch companies sailed to the East Indies themselves for spices and other merchandise. Grand Pensionary Johan van Oldenbarneveldt (1547-1619) decided to unite the various companies into a single United East Indies Company, so that the Republic would become strong both militarily and economically. The VOC conquered Spanish and Portuguese harbors and forts in the East and set up new trading posts. As it turned out, the VOC would rule the overseas trade for nearly two centuries, from the Cape of Good Hope to Japan. When the French grabbed the power from the Republic in 1799, the VOC was disbanded.
In its time, the VOC was the largest trading company in the world.

"In the Sinterklaas period, the Dutch eat what they call pepper nuts. Everybody thinks that's very Dutch, but I was interested to discover that they owe this treat to the VOC [the United East Indies Company] and commonly known as the Dutch East India Company. I wanted such a return ship in the book rather than a museum ship. I wanted one under full sail."

The special flavour of pepper nuts comes from the eastern spices: pepper, cardamom, aniseed, caraway, cinnamon, nutmeg, and clove. These costly spices were transported to the Netherlands by the VOC. In those days, the Dutch used the word "pepper" for spices in general.

DUTCH SPECIALTIES

"If an illustration contains a smaller illustration of itself that keeps repeating, then we call it the 'Droste effect,' seen here because of the illustration on this cocoa tin. A Droste tin like this stood in my mother's kitchen in France throughout my childhood so I had to include it."

Jan Misset (1871-1931), a painter living in Haarlem, designed the Droste tin in 1904.
Gerardus Johannes Droste opened his confectionery business in 1863 in Haarlem. The products made there, including the "Pastilles Droste," chocolate discs, were such a success that the first Droste chocolate and cocoa factory was opened in 1890. Droste is still the largest chocolate manufacturer in the Netherlands.

NURSERY RHYME

There was once a little girl
Who wanted to sail
Who wanted to sail
There was once a little girl
Who wanted to sail as a sailor

(folk song)

FLYING DUTCHMAN

"The sea immediately reminded me of the story of the Flying Dutchman—a transparent ghost ship that sailed against the wind with full sail. For me, that was something nice to paint."

A Dutch captain of a VOC ship wanted to set sail quickly in order to make as much profit as possible. It was Easter Sunday and a storm was raging, and sailing on such a holy day was prohibited. Yet, the captain still decided to leave, "Even if I have to sail throughout eternity!" he cried. Those who came to see the ship off saw, to their horror, how it departed into the wind, under full sail that glowed red. It never returned.
Later stories were told by seamen who had seen a ghost ship near the Cape of Good Hope. It was sailing into the wind, its sails full and glowing red—The Flying Dutchman.

WHALE HUNT

In the 17th century, the Dutch hunted whales near Spitsbergen to process them for cod liver oil. They were so active that this species of whale had almost died out by 1670. The Dutch also tried other places, but nowhere else was as successful. The Dutch finally stopped hunting whales in 1873.

"Night has turned into day. We are getting closer to the coast of Zeeland and it's raining. It does that a lot in Holland. If you're unlucky, there'll be lots of wind as well, especially in your face.
At sea, Michiel de Ruyter beat the English, and that was quite an achievement because the English were really good sailors. I had to include that victory in the book. For me, it's great to paint the aftermath of such a sea battle. All I had to do was to find out what one ship looked like and then I could make do with sinking masts and the odd flag."

THE SEA NEAR HOLLAND DAY

SHIP

"When I was working on this picture, my other half came into my studio and said, 'Charlotte, did you know that the newest frigate of the Dutch navy is called The Seven Provinces just like Michiel de Ruyter's flagship?' 'Got you,' I thought, 'you're mine!'"
The frigate The Seven Provinces, was taken into service in 2002. It is over 470 feet long and 57 feet wide. It is fitted with machine guns, a cannon, rockets, torpedoes, two interceptors, and a helicopter. It served in the Enduring Freedom operation and was also deployed against pirates off the coast of Somalia.

'This is one of today's fishing vessels from Urk—notice the letters UK. Everything today is automated. The trawling nets that drag the bottom of the sea was something they didn't have in the past.'
This fishing boat has nets on both sides. The nets are dragged through the water and the fish are scooped up.

"Michiel de Ruyter had a ship named the Seven Provinces. I had to research what it looked like in aspect because there are children who know every detail about things like that and immediately see if you get something wrong."
The Seven Provinces was built in Rotterdam in 1664-1665, The ship was around 150 feet long and 40 feet wide, had eighty cannon and more than 21,500 square feet of sail. It was Michiel de Ruyter's flagship. After the death of De Ruyter, the ship was scuppered in 1692 in a war against the French. Two years later, it went to the broker's yard.

"This is a bomschuit, an old Dutch fishing vessel that was designed to ride the waves. It was a really beautiful vessel, completely round and very flat. These boats would take to the sea, but could not go far because it was too dangerous. This vessel is from Scheveningen as shown by the letters SCH."
A flat bottom vessel has little or no keel. This means it can sail in very shallow water. They can easily be beached and this makes them perfect for shell fishers.

"The Dutch haven't fought the English for centuries. To underline that, I've shown the Stena Line, which connects the two countries. That brings a bit of balance to history."
Stena Line has been operating the ferry service between the Netherlands and Great Britain since 1989. The Stena Hollandica and Stena Britannica both sail back and forth each day between Hoek van Holland and Harwich with passengers and freight.

THE DELTA WORKS

"This is a section of the Haringvliet Dam. The fight against water is something that's fundamentally part of being Dutch. The Delta Works, of which the Haringvliet Dam is a part, was the Dutch response to the floods of 1953."
The Haringvliet Dam encloses the Haringvliet. It was built between 1961 and 1971 and is more than three miles long. There are seventeen locks, and together these can allow 88,000 cubic feet of water per second to flow through.

C MICHIEL DE RUYTER
(1607-1676)
SEA HEROES AND THE
BROAD SCOPE OF THE
REPUBLIC

"I wanted to include in every illustration a figure who could actually appear in it. What do you see at sea? Seagulls! That's why Charlie with the Wooden Leg is flying around here."

Charlie with the Wooden Leg is a character from *Tow-Truck Pluck* written by Annie M.G. Schmidt and illustrated by Fiep Westendorp. It first appeared as a serial in *Margriet* magazine between 1968 and 1970. *Tow-Truck Pluck* was published as a book in 1971.

Michiel de Ruyter first boarded a ship at the age of 11 as boatswain's lad. He grew into privateer, rear admiral, and merchant seaman.

By his 45th birthday, he had earned enough to retire but was quickly asked to return to the navy to fight the English. He ended up with the rank of Lieutenant Admiral and achieved considerable success during battles in the Anglo-Dutch wars.

De Ruyter achieved his greatest success on the open sea in the Four Days' Battle from 11 to 14 June 1666. During the battle, seventeen English ships were sunk while the Dutch only lost four.

In 1667, he defeated a large section of the English fleet in the Medway near Chatham. Nine years later, he died in the fight against the French.

WIC

After the founding of the VOC (see p.3), the West Indies Company (WIC) was founded in 1921 based on the same idea. The WIC traded in West Africa, America and with all the islands between America and New Guinea.

In 1674, the first WIC went into bankruptcy. Five years later, the second WIC was founded, concentrating mainly on the trade in slaves and gold. This company ended in 1792.

"Piet Hein learned to knit when he was a rowing slave and was not allowed to leave the ship. Knitting passed the time. When he reached the rank of lieutenant admiral, he still knitted socks for his crew members."

Piet Hein (1577-1629) was lieutenant admiral and commander of the West Indies Company.

He is particularly famous for the conquest of the Spanish treasure fleet in 1628.

Every year, the Spanish treasure fleet would carry valuable shipments from the Spanish colonies to Spain. In 1628, Piet Hein succeeded in capturing a number of these ships. The profits, 177,000 pounds of silver and thousands of pearls, were enough to fund the war against Spain for a whole year.

"Before I began, I didn't realize I would have to research absolutely everything. Take something as simple as a seagull. What sorts of seagulls fly around Holland? You might think a seagull is a seagull. But no, there are many different breeds. That's what makes it so special."

The seagull with the black head is called black-headed gull and the one with black tips to its wings is a silver gull.

"Here's another one: Brave Ben by my friend Mies van Hout."

The picture book *Brave Ben* was written by Mathilde Stein and illustrated by Mies van Hout. It first appeared in 2005.

Did you hear of the silver fleet
The silver fleet of Spain?
There were lots of Spanish mats on board
And apples of Orange!
Piet Hein! Piet Hein! Piet Hein his name is small
His deeds are great, his deeds are great
He beat the silver fleet
He beat, he beat the silver fleet.

(composition: J.J. Viotta, text: J.P. Heije, 1844)

"At first, I had the flags on the ships blowing the wrong way. I thought that if the ship sailed forwards, the flag would blow to the rear. But that's all wrong of course: the wind comes from behind and fills the sails and also blows all the flags forward."

During the Eighty Years' War (1568-1648) there wasn't one uniform Dutch flag. Each flag had orange/red, white and blue stripes, but the number and order changed.

"I didn't start the book on 1 January, because the sea is naturally at its best in the summer, when everybody can enjoy a paddle. I racked my brains and puzzled about everything until New Year came right in the middle of the book.
We arrive at the coast. Behind the high dune you can see the dunes of Holland. The publisher said, 'You can make it into a wonderfully quiet spot.' Quiet? There are horse trails, hiking trails, bicycle paths, everywhere there are signs telling you where to go, explanation signs, etc. 'Quiet' simply didn't work. You won't find any real quiet anywhere in this book. Holland is organized down to the square inch."

THE DUNES EARLY JULY

FUN ON THE BEACH

"The beach houses that people rent in the summer are something typically Dutch. They are placed on the beach in two or three rows and people can more or less live in them for the whole summer. These houses are actually far too close together, so this gives rise to arguments about the boundaries, which is again typically Dutch: they argue about where their land stops and the next person's begins and so on."

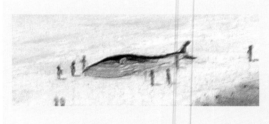

"Occasionally a whale will wash ashore. I've included it for the children, because it's really very exciting."

"On the beach, they often hold sandcastle competitions."

"There is a special swimsuit known as the burkini for Muslim women who can't go to the beach with their body exposed."
The burkini is a swimsuit with long sleeves, long legs and a scarf for the head. It was designed by the Lybian-Australian Aheda Zanetti and was introduced throughout the world in 2007.

"To create an exotic ambiance, they plant palm trees near some beach tents. Holland doesn't have exotic beaches, but you can relax here. A palm tree simply can't survive in Holland, so they've all died and are now secured by ropes so that they don't blow over."

NURSERY RHYME

"Children sometimes celebrate their birthday by the sea with cake. They sing songs and play games, such as here, 'I wrote a letter to my mother.'"

I wrote a letter to my mother
And on the way
I dropped it
And one of you
has picked it up
And put it in their pocket

Children sing the song while sitting in a circle. One of the children walks around the circle with a handkerchief. When the song stops, he places the handkerchief behind the child where he's standing at the moment. That child then gets up and tries to tag the first one before he has run around the circle and taken the vacant place.

PAINTINGS

"The Dutch have organized everything in the dunes. There's a notice at every path, saying what it is intended for and what you can and cannot do. Here you can walk, here you can cycle, but don't mix them up!"

"In this illustration, you will find various paintings. I am particularly fond of this painting by Jozef Israëls. It hangs on the wall of my studio. It is fake, of course since the original hangs in the Rijksmuseum."
Jozef Israëls (1824-1911), *Children of the Sea* (1872)

"Horses pulling vessels in and out of the sea in the past was typically Dutch. I based this drawing on a painting by Mauve. He often illustrated such a vessel with horses, except that he would paint the scene from the front."
Anton Mauve (1838-1888)

"If I show a painting by Jozef Israëls, then I also have to include something by his son Isaac. Isaac was somewhat more modern in approach and style. He painted these donkeys by the sea where rich children at the time could take a ride on a donkey for a few pennies. This boy kept the donkeys moving."
Isaac Israëls (1865-1934), *Donkey Rides Along the Beach* (ca. 1890-1901)

FIGURES FROM CHILDREN'S LITERATURE

"Something else typically Dutch are the pillars on the beach for children who become separated from their parents so that they can find each other.
The pillars sport figures by Dick Bruna. One is Miffy, and this little man is, I believe, nameless."
Dick Bruna (1927) thought up the first Miffy story for his son during a holiday on the Dutch coast. It appeared in 1955, with the title *Nijntje* (*Miffy*). Altogether, thirty books have appeared in the series.

WORLD WAR II

"I wanted to show something of the history in every illustration. But what on earth could I show in the dunes? Suddenly it came to me! There are bunkers from the Second World War!"

C **WORLD WAR II**
(1940-1945)
OCCUPATION AND LIBERATION
On 10 May 1940, the Germans entered the Netherlands. The Dutch army was out-of-date and far too weak to repel the attack. After the bombing of Rotterdam on 14 May, Holland surrendered. Dutch men were put to work in Germany. Jews, gypsies, homosexuals, and people from the resistance were sent to concentration camps. More than 100,000 never

returned. In the autumn of 1944, the south of Holland was liberated by the allied forces (Canadians, Americans, and English). The northern part of the Netherlands suffered a terrible winter of famine, during which tens of thousands of people died.
After the German surrender on 4 May 1945, all of the Netherlands was liberated.

"I saw a poster hanging on a bridge near us for the musical Soldaat van Oranje [Soldier of Orange]. That was the perfect solution: I could show the resistance and the musical—because that, too, has become part of Dutch culture—in one fell

swoop. It was also was rather nice that when Holland was published, I was invited by the producer to attend the musical. It was wonderful!"
Erik Hazelhoff Roelfzema was a student when World War II broke out. In 1941, he fled to England after he had spoken out against the occupier in a manifesto. He regularly traveled to Holland to deliver broadcasting equipment to the resistance and to pick up refugees. He later became a pilot with the RAF and carried out bombing flights to Germany. He ended up as adjutant to Queen Wilhelmina. After the war he described his experiences in a book that appeared under the title *Soldaat van Oranje* (*Soldier of Orange*, 1971) and was succesfully filmed in 1979 by Paul Verhoeven (1938).

"The Dutch want to tell everybody about everything and warn them against it. Here there is a board with an explanation about ticks—that you should be careful, that they can make you sick, how you can avoid such a tick, and what you should do if you are bitten."

"Don't worry: you'll never lose your way in Holland. There are signs everywhere."

SAIL

"This sailboat is my way of dealing with Sail Amsterdam. There's a poster in Amsterdam, but I couldn't get the whole show on it. This sailboat is on its way to the IJ."
Sail Amsterdam has been held every five years since 1975. Large sail ships, modern ships, marine ships, and replicas of historic ships come from all over the world to Amsterdam harbor where people can view them.

WIND PARK

"In Holland, you find windmills everywhere. Both the old and the new had to have a place in this book."
The Princess Amalia Windpark off the coast near IJmuiden was opened in 2008 and has 60 windmills.

RACING

In the dunes of Zandvoort you can also find the Circuit Park Zandvoort. The first race on this circuit, the Zandvoort Grand Prix, was held in 1948. The shape and length of the circuit has been changed several times, and since 1999 it has become 4.3 kilometres long. Formula 1 races were held here between 1952 and 1985. Nowadays, races are organized for both cars and motorbikes.

NOT MADE-UP

This roundabout with a map of Holland can be found in Vlijmen.

"These are the five inhabited Dutch wadden islands: Texel, Vlieland, Terschelling, Ameland, and Schiermonnikoog. My other half and I went island hopping from Texel to Vlieland and Terschelling to see the differences and similarities between these islands.
If I had drawn the islands exactly as they are, this illustration would have become a tourist folder. What's more, if I had shown all five islands from a bird's eye view, everything would have been so small that there would be nothing interesting to see. That's why I decided to stick the islands together."

SECOND HALF OF JULY

THE FIVE WADDEN ISLANDS

WILLEM BARENTSZ

"Willem Barentsz was born on Terschelling, but how on earth could I make that clear? I couldn't show his Behouden Huys (Safe House)—another piece of history—in Holland, because it's actually on Nova Zembla. I found another way. The Terschellings Museum 't Behouden Huys has a reconstruction of the original Behouden Huys. Inside there are also rooms decorated in the style of the times with men and women in costume. I have two of those women take a walk outside with their children."

Explorer Willem Barentsz (c. 1550-1597) tried to find a northerly passage to the East. In 1596, he sailed past Nova Zembla, but he became trapped in the ice. He used the wood from his ship to build a house where he and his crew could spend the winter, the "Behouden Huys" (Safe House). When the weather improved and a thaw set in, he used driftwood to build a boat in which the seventeen survivors could sail home. But just a week after their departure, he died. The rest of the crew reached the inhabited world alive.

THE ISLANDS

You arrive there in the evening after a long boat trip. The sun is setting and your family has rented a house or reserved a spot at a campground. You set off with all your stuff on your back, your cases on wheels, and your bear. When you finally reach the final destination—and by now you're slightly weary—then the real holiday can begin."

TEXEL

VLIELAND

AMELAND

SCHIERMONNIKOOG

RACING

"On Texel they've got small carts that you can race over the island in. I thought that would be fun, but unfortunately they were closed when we were on the island."

DRILLING

In 1967, the first Dutch drilling platform, Sedneth I, was launched in the North Sea. It drilled for the Royal—Shell Group. Today, more than 140 Dutch drilling platforms are located in the North Sea to produce gas and oil.

FIGURES FROM CHILDREN'S LITERATURE

"These are Spekkie and Sproet, by my friend Juliette de Wit with a story by Vivian den Hollander."

The first story about the detectives Spekkie (Marshmallow) and Sproet (Freckle) appeared in a reading method series *Spekkie en Sproet en de gestolen auto* (*Marshmallow and Freckle and the Stolen Car*, 1999).

SAGAS AND LEGENDS

"Every island has its own statue. On Terschelling there is the Stryper woman."
In 1666, the English attacked Terschelling. After they had plundered West Terschelling, they moved eastwards. Near a small place called Striep, they came across an old woman whom they asked what could be found further away. She indicated the Stryper cemetery in the distance and said: "They stand in their hundreds but lie there in their thousands."
The English, who thought she was talking about a Terschelling hoard laying in wait for them, turned and fled.
The statue *The Stryper Woman* (1982) stands between Baaiduinen and Striep and was made by Huib Noorlander (1928-2004).

"I thought at first that only Terschelling had such a statue, but do you know what? Ameland also has such a woman."
The statue is of Rixt van Oerd, also called the "Witch of Oerd".
Rixt lived with her son Sjoerd on Oerd in the dunes of Ameland. They survived on whatever they could scavenge, but Sjoerd thought that life was too hard and he went to sea.
Once, he failed to come home from one of his voyages. Rixt had to return to scavenging for her upkeep, but not enough was washed ashore. One night, she tied her lantern high in the dune so that ships would think it was a lighthouse. Her plan succeeded: one ship ran aground on a sandbank, broke into pieces, and a rich cargo was washed onto the shore.

The next morning, there was also a body on the beach. It was Sjoerd who had been on the lost ship on his way home.

"On Schiermonnikoog there is a statue of a monk."
Schier is an old Dutch word for "gray". Schiermonnikoog literally means "the island [*oog*] of the grey monks."
Around 1166, Cistercian monks moved from Friesland to Schiermonnikoog. They founded a chapel there, kept cattle, and tilled the land.
The statue *The Grey Monk* (1961) was made by the painter-sculptor Martin van Waning (1887-1972).

RHINO

"They have a wonderful museum on Texel that contains a reconstruction of a long-haired rhinoceros from prehistoric times. Somebody complained and asked why I had drawn that creature on this picture. Go to the museum and you'll see why. On Texel, they have fences along the meadows. That was great for me, because it allowed me to put the rhinoceros in a different field from the sheep. It wouldn't be very nice if they got too close to each other."
The hairy rhinoceros lived about 40,000 years ago in Holland. It was around ten feet long and five feet tall. It went extinct 13,000 years ago.

NATURE

"I had to include these sandbanks with seals on them because children love seals."

In Holland, there are two seal shelters where sick or wounded seals can recover until they are able to swim independently. On Texel, seals have been cared for since 1952, and in Pieterburen since 1971. The Dutch coast is divided between these two shelters, so that every seal washed ashore can be immediately taken to the right place.

Ecomare on Texel gives information about the wadden area and the North Sea. It consists of a natural museum, a seal refuge centre, a sea aquarium, a bird refuge, a dune park, and a visitors' center.

THE LIGHTHOUSES

1   2   3   4   5

1 The lighthouse on Terschelling is around 175 feet high and is called the Brandaris, named after Saint Brandarius or Brandanus, the patron saint against fire. It is Terschelling's third lighthouse and dates from 1594. The first, from 1323, collapsed into the sea in 1592. The second was so badly built that it fell down just after it was completed.
The Brandaris is the oldest lighthouse in Holland. In 1837, it became the first lighthouse with a revolving lens and in 1907 it was converted to run on electricity. Nowadays, the lighthouse is completely automatic.

"Somebody remarked: 'That's not fair: you've done the lighthouse of Terschelling, but what about the others?'
Well, I had to do something so I've made advertising boards for Vlieland, Texel, and Schiermonnikoog showing lighthouses."
2 The Vlieland lighthouse, the Vuurduin (Fire Dune), has shone since 1909 from the Vuurboetsduin. Before then, it stood in IJmuiden. It is only 55 feet tall, but because it stands on a dune, it shines nearly 200 feet above sea level.
The Vuurduin was designed by architect Quirinus Harder (1801-1880) who also designed the lighthouses on Texel and Ameland, and and dates from 1876.

3 The Eierland lighthouse on Texel stands on a dune that is around 65 feet high. Because of that, the light shines 175 feet above sea. It has been in operation since 1864.
4 Bornrif is the name given to the lighthouse that Quirinus Harder designed for Ameland. It was put into service in 1880. After the Second World War, it was nicknamed "the Table Lamp," because of its weak light. Since 1952, it has shone at full strength again.
5 The Noordertoren (North Tower) on Schiermonnikoog was designed by architect H.G. Jansen and has been in operation since 1854. It was not painted red until 1998.

BAAAAAAAA

"There are lots of sheep on Texel so you have sheep's wool, sheep's blankets, and much more, so I had to put them in. They breed a very special sheep here known as the Texelaar. Those sheep have very broad heads. I really did my best to get this just right, but in the end you don't see a lot of it."
There are just as many sheep on Texel as people. The Texelaar is raised for its wool and meat. Every year, around 11,000 lambs are born on the island.

HISTORY

They even constructed a channel from Kampen to Terschelling so that cogs could sail without hindrance.

Here, Cor Adema is standing in front of the ship, his green beret on his head. The building in the background is called 'the castle'. It looks like one, too."

The cogs sailed from around 1200 to c. 1450. The Kampen Cog is a reconstruction of a wreck from

"This is a cog—an odd ship without a keel. That makes it difficult to sail.

The cog originally comes from Kampen. You can see it again in the picture in this book of Kampen. There, they have copied the historic ship, and I spoke to the man behind it all, Cor Adema, by telephone.

When we went to the harbor on Terschelling, the cog was moored there. Suddenly I saw a man, and I thought, 'That must be Adema.' And he said, 'You're Charlotte!' I asked him what he was doing with the cog on Terschelling and he explained that this ship always sailed to Terschelling.

1336. Four years were spent on its construction.

The Cog does not have to pay any harbor fees on Terchelling—that is an ancient right because in 1323 Kampen donated all the building materials for the first lighthouse on Terschelling. The exemption used to apply to all vessels from Kampen. Today, only the wooden ships from Kampen enjoy this right.

"On Ameland, there is an arch made from two mammoth tusks that were found there."

Mammoths lived here when the North Sea was still dry land (until about 8000 years ago). A piece of a mammoth bone was found on the beach of Ameland in 2011.

TRADITIONS AND FESTIVALS

"They hold a sloop race on Terschelling, but it's taking things a bit too far to draw all those boats."

During the sloop race, people row in lifeboats that were originally on ships. It is a sport that is practiced virtually exclusively in Holland. The sloop race between Harlingen and Terschelling is held each year on the Friday after Ascension Day. The distance raced is around 35 kilometers.

Since 1981, Oerol, an annual ten-day cultural festival is held every June on Terschelling. The island location is the starting point when programming the music, theatre and visual arts. The Oerol on Terschelling is now one of the largest and most reputable location theater festivals in the world.

"There are some crazy Dutch people who go mudflat hiking. When the tide is out, they walk from the mainland to the island. It seems scary to me... but courageous too! I saw some photos where things went wrong and all at once, they're up to their waist in seawater because the tide has suddenly turned. It is not without danger."

When it's low tide, you can walk from the mainland to Ameland, Schiermonnikoog, or Rottumeroog. Mudflat hiking has been popular since the '1960s.

"On Ameland and Terschelling, lifeboats are launched into the sea by a team of horses. I thought one is just fine. Let's not exaggerate."

In Ameland, a lifeboat has been pulled into the waves by horses since 1824. On Terschelling, the last horse-drawn life boat was launched in 1950, but the tradition was revived in 2010 as a tourist attraction.

THE DUTCH SPECIALTIES

"Anyone coming to Terschelling will immediately rent a bike and perhaps go and eat some fish in the harbor."

The Dutch *lekkerbek* is a fillet of fish that used to be whiting or cod, but nowadays is almost always hake which is battered and deep fried.

Kibbeling, which is derived from *kabeljauwwang* (cod cheeks), is the name for small pieces of white fish (such as cob, hake, whiting or pollack), battered and deep fried.

Hollandse Nieuwe, (new herring) or *Maatjesharing* (which is derived from the Dutch word for virgin herring), is the first young herring of the season which are cleaned, salted, and filleted.

"The Spar is a supermarket located on the island's camp sites. It really does belong here."

The Spar was founded in 1932 in Zoetermeer by Adriaan van Well (1898-1967). The name is said to mean "through harmonious collaboration all profit regularly" (in Dutch, the initials spell out De Spar), but it is also said that the founder drew a fir tree (a "*spar*" in Dutch) on the minutes of the constituent meeting. Today, Spar is an international chain with around 12,500 branches.

The story goes that in 1839, barrels were washed ashore on Terschelling containing hard red berries. Beachcombers who didn't know what to do with them threw them away. On that spot, cranberry plants started to grow. It was not until around 1900 that the islanders discovered that the berries tasted rather good. Initially, the cranberries were mainly exported to England. Today, everybody throughout Holland knows that this berry is both delicious and healthy.

The c1000 supermarkets have only been around since 1981 under that name, but began in 1888 in Groningen. It was there that Jacob Fokke Schuitema opened a grocery shop and wholesale business that was later taken over by his two nephews.

The nephews were able to form an alliance with an additional twelve wholesalers and they called themselves Schuitema and Centra. They continued to grow until the end of the1970s. When shoppers started to turn to cheaper competitors, c1000 was created—cheaper shops with independent entrepreneurs in charge. There are now around 400 c1000 shops in Holland.

TRANSPORT OPTIONS

De Vliehors is an artillery training ground on Vlieland. It is used for practice with bomb throwers, rockets, and shooting at ground targets. The navy holds exercises in the western part of the Wadden Sea, in particularly off Texel, where the Joost Dourlein Barracks are located and where the navy specializes in amphibian knowledge.

The ferry to Texel leaves from Den Helder, to Vlieland and Terschelling from Harlingen, to Ameland from Holwerd and to Schiermonnikoog from Lauwersoog. You can't take cars onto Vlieland and Schiermonnikoog.

The North Sea is one of the busiest seas in the world. Every year, there are some 260,000 shipping movements through the Dutch part of the North Sea. Container ships are required to keep to fixed routes. It is not unusual for containers to be swept overboard (it happens to about 10,000 worldwide every year) and many are washed up on the wadden islands.

ARCHITECTURE

A sheepfold on Texel is called *skiipeboete* locally. Although the word suggests otherwise, virtually no sheep ever stand in the sheepfolds on Texel. They stay outside as much as possible, and the folds are used for storing hay and to give the ewes a place to have their lambs.

The reformed church of Den Hoorn on Texel dates from 1425. The tower was added in 1450 and for a long time it served as a beacon for shipping.

The Texelse Oudheidkamer (Antiquity Chamber). The building dates from 1599 and was formerly a lodging house. Over the door is written"

He who closes his ears to the pleas of the poor shall receive no compassion from God.

Today it is a museum, completely furnished in the style of the 19th century.

Characteristic monument building in Den Burg on Texel with a bevelled façade.

"This is a really beautiful house, much more beautiful than what I've drawn here. It used to provide shelter for orphans and the widows of men who drowned at sea. The idea was that seamen who returned safely should donate a small portion of their profit to the house. In this way, they kept the island alive together."

The Diaconiehuis (Deacon's House) on Vlieland, known as the 'Armhuis' (House of the Poor) has existed in its present form since 1678. It also offered housing to the elderly and provided care to those washed ashore.

Above the entrance there is a sign from 1732 with the text:

**In this place, destitute men and women are
Endowed with the charity owed to the poor
The orphan also finds his home in this place
Show your generosity as a witness to all duty
They all pray friendly to you when they are in need
For one small gift, and God for our daily bread.**

*"This is a very pretty house that stands right on the north coast of Vlieland on the sand flats. It is built on pillars, so that the water can flow under it when the beach is covered at high tide.
A shipwreck survivor who is able to reach the beach can shelter here. If he raises the flag on the mast, they can see from inland that there is a survivor and they come and get him at low tide."*

The survivors' house is partly constructed of driftwood. The area around it is currently used as an exercise area by the military, and the house is now a beachcomber museum. You can visit it when the military are not holding exercises.

"These two buildings are in Nes on Ameland. The one in the front is one of the oldest houses on Ameland and was built in 1625."

**Pussy dear
Come on here
I've got some tasty milk to share
And for me
Strawberry tea
Tasty treats for you and me**

FINE ARTS

"Here, I've paid homage to Isings by showing a small piece of one of his school posters, depicting the Behouden Huys."
J.H. Isings (1884-1977), *Behouden Huys on Nova Zembla* is a watercolor painting that was printed up for schools between 1950 and 1953. According to the painter, his illustration shows the events of 29 May 1597. Willem Barentsz wrote about this in his diary.

ROTTERDAM   FIRST HALF OF AUGUST

THE HARBOUR

C THE HARBOUR OF ROTTERDAM
(vanaf ca. 1880)
GATE TO THE WORLD

Around 1250, the river the Rotte was separated by a dam from the sea water, so that the river would not become salty. At this spot, goods were transferred from river ships to sea-worthy coastal vessels.

In the 16th century, the Rotterdam's harbor developed into an important fishing port, but the most important harbor for colonial goods was still Amsterdam.

Between 1866 and 1872, the Nieuwe Waterweg (New Waterway) was dug. It provided a better connection between the harbor of Rotterdam and the North Sea, and in the years that followed, it was widened and deepened. Rotterdam acquired a direct link with the mining and industrial areas in the Ruhr area in Germany. From that moment, the harbor growth was spectacular. After the damage from Second World War, it was crucial for the Dutch economy that the harbor was rebuilt as quickly as possible.

The port of Rotterdam is the most important container harbor in Europe. Annually, around 96,000 inland waterway vessels and 34,000 seafaring ships arrive here, together responsible for more than 430 million tons in goods transshipment. The industrial area has five oil refineries, six biofuel factories, four gasfired generating plants, seventy wind turbines, and forty-five chemical companies.

"In the port of Rotterdam, they work with a type of lifting machine to place or remove containers on a ship. The truck has a magnet that fastens itself to the container. The container is then lifted and placed on the ship. It is highly precise work but sometimes a truck parks under the lifting machine and they forget to release the container. When the magnet comes near, it doesn't only lift the container, but also the truck and everybody in it. I thought that was a great story so here the machine has lifted my friend Geert-Jan

into the air, even though in reality that could never happen because his car is made of plastic."

These warehouses used to store goods from the Dutch colonies. The names on the warehouses explain where the stored goods originated.

BRIDGES

"Holland has a lot of water and that means a lot of bridges. You'd think they'd keep things simple and stick to one type of bridge, but instead they have all sorts. This, for example, is a vertical lift bridge."

Officially, this bridge by architect Pieter Joosting (1867-1942) is called the Koningshavenbrug (King's Harbor Bridge), but every Rotterdammer calls this old railway lifting bridge "The Lift." It was opened in 1927 and was the first bridge of its kind in Western Europe. It was decommissioned in 1993, but it still remains a landmark in Rotterdam.

Ben van Berkel (1957) designed the Erasmus Bridge over the New Maas, which connects the city center with the southern district. The bridge is the largest and heaviest bascule bridge in Western Europe to allow large ships to pass. Shortly after its opening in 1996, it was discovered that the road surface would start to sway in winds of six on the Beaufort Scale. The problem was quickly solved. The nickname for the Erasmus Bridge is "The Swan."

Cor Veerling (1926) designed the red Willems bridge—as replacement for the old Willems bridge— which was opened in 1981 by Willem-Alexander, when he was still prince. Because everything had to be as cheap as possible, the bridge was one yard lower than planned and its construction took no less than six years. The bridge connects the right bank of the New Maas with the Noordereiland (North Island).

In 1965, Queen Juliana opened the Van Brienenoord Bridge, named after the Island of Brienenoord which is below it. The design, which was considered uniquely elegant at the time, was by W.J. van der Eb (1904-1966). The bridge carries one of the the busiest motorways in Holland. Very soon after its opening, the Van Brienenoord Bridge became infamous for its traffic jams. In 1990, a second bridge, identical to the first, was opened alongside it, allowing the traffic to move more freely.

ERASMUS

C ERASMUS (ca. 1496-1536)

*"Rotterdam is famous for Erasmus.
You see his portrait everywhere."*

AN INTERNATIONAL HUMANIST

Desiderius Erasmus was probably an illegitimate child of a priest. He was educated in a monastery and studied mainly the classics and the Italian humanists—thinkers who believed that people were not controlled by God but rather were responsible for their own deeds and that everybody had the right to a good life. After Erasmus was ordained as priest, he traveled throughout Europe and continued to study and write. In his best known book, *The Praise of Folly*, he wrote how people are concerned primarily with themselves and judge others negatively. In his later life, he became advisor to Emperor Charles V and founded the Three Language College in Leuven, where lessons were given in Greek, Latin, and Hebrew.

LEMNISCAAT

"This is my publisher."
Lemniscaat Publishers was founded in 1963 by Jean Louis and Marijke Boele van Hensbroek and in 1986 taken over by their son Jean Christophe.
The publishing house specializes in picture books, books for children and young people, and books about philosophy.

BOATS

The Port Police—previously called the River Police—has been active since 1895. Initially the organization was responsible for border control, keeping the peace, and assistance in the harbor. With the growth of the harbor, international criminal detection became a necessary additional duty.
Police equipment can be recognized by the fluorescent orange-red and reflecting blue stripes on a white background.

The Port Police has various types of police launches including this super-fast and maneuverable model.

The *Abel Tasman* is the flagship of the Spido fleet, which operates excursions through the Rotterdam harbors.
The ship is named after the explorer Abel Janszoon Tasman (1603-1659) who discovered New Zealand, Tonga, the Fiji Islands and later Tasmania.

A special ferry service with small water taxis operates between the Hotel New York, the Veerhaven, and the Leuvehaven.

The *Port of Rotterdam* is the firefloat (officially: "Incident combating and patrol vessel") of the Rotterdam Port Authority.

Between 1873 and 1978, there was a regular sea connection between Rotterdam and New York operated by the Holland-America Line. It was formerly the most important way for emigrants and travelers to reach America. Later, when flying became cheaper, the ships were used for cruises.
This is the SS Rotterdam, which was in service from 1901 to 1929 and offered accommodation to 2,282 passengers.

THE BOMBING

"The bombing of Rotterdam in the Second World War is commemorated by a sculpture by Zadkine, a statue of a man without a heart."
Ossip Zadkine (1890-1967), *The Devastated City* (1953). Zadkine got the idea for the sculpture when he traveled through Rotterdam by train on a railway line that no longer exists and saw how the heart of the city had been literally blown away.

"Somebody told me: 'Charlotte, if you show the Zadkine statue, don't forget to draw the response to it. Wherever any construction takes place, the hoarding always shows the same message: "Listen, here beats Rotterdam's new heart."'"
Since 2008, the campaign "Listen, here beats Rotterdam's new heart," has provided an artistic theme for all the building sites that are (still) found in the city.

DUTCH SPECIALTIES

In 1781, Johannes van Nelle and his wife opened a shop in Rotterdam specializing in coffee, tea, tobacco, and "snuis" (snuff tobacco). Over the years, they started their own plantations for tobacco, coffee, and tea.
Since 1989, Van Nelle has been owned by Sara Lee/Douwe Egberts. The characteristic red-yellow advertising for Van Nelle was designed in 1930 by Jac. Jongert (1883-1942).

Baker's son Anton ter Beek (1877-1958) specialized around the turn of the century in baking rusks. In 1954, his sons opened a rusk factory. They called it "Bolletje" after the balls of dough that are produced to make rusks. Today, Bolletje has three factories and produces other baked goods, but the company remains famous for its rusks.

The advertising slogan "I want Bolletje" was awarded as the Dutch advertising slogan of the 20th century.

ON THE BEACH

"The city beach is a new phenomenon in Holland. You can go and lie on the beach right in the middle of the city."

DESIGN

Customs van. The vehicles of the police, customs, fire service, ambulance, royal military police, and the emergency services have special stripes known as BKZ stripes, designed in 1992 by Studio Dumbar in Rotterdam. Each service has its own color. Customs, for example, has yellow with green stripes on a white vehicle.

RASCALS

"I really wanted to include a prison in the book, because you naturally have those in Holland too. Not everybody stays on the straight and narrow. Actually, I had originally planned the prison on the illustration with the mist, but then it literally disappeared in the mist. That's why a Justice Prison Service bus carrying a scoundrel is driving over the bridge."

A POPULATION OF MANY HUES

"More than half of the population of Rotterdam comes from countries other than Holland. I counted everything carefully so that there are more people of color in the illustration than white people."

C A HOLLAND OF MANY HUES (from 1945)

THE MULTICULTURAL SOCIETY

After the Second World War, many immigrants came to Holland especially from the former Dutch colony of Indonesia. In the '60s, "guest workers" were brought from countries including Italy, Spain, Yugoslavia, Turkey and Morocco. Holland also offered refuge to political refugees from a wide range of countries. In 1955, Holland's first mosque was founded. Since the close of the '1980s, special Hindu and Islamic education has also been available.
In 1995, the Dutch borders were opened to people from European countries that had signed the Schengen Agreement.
The prediction is that by 2050,

30% of the total population of Holland will be of non-Dutch origin.

CARNAVAL

"In Rotterdam, an exotic carnival is held every year. What amuses me is that they celebrate at the end of July, the month which, according to the VVV [Dutch Tourist Office], has the most rainfall."
The Street Parade of the Summer Carnival is held on the last Saturday in July, and it is the summer counterpart to the Dutch carnival in February. The immigrants from Latin America and the Cape Verde Islands celebrate their own tropical carnival on that day.

"A multicultural society automatically means all sorts of foreign restaurants. Everything is all mixed up together and that is not a problem. That's why I've shown a Suriname sandwich shop, a Moroccan eating house, a Vietnamese loempia stall, African food and a döner kebab takeaway."
In Holland there are more foreign restaurants than Dutch or French. In fact, 18% of all restaurants are Chinese-Indonesian and 9% are Italian.

26 MILES AND 385 YARDS

"These two runners are already in training for the Rotterdam Marathon. Since the Kenyans generally win, they're running here as well—they're the best athletes."
The Rotterdam Marathon has been held every year since 1981, generally in April. It is the largest marathon in Holland—followed by the Amsterdam Marathon—and one of the most popular marathons in the world.

SEASONS

"Since I move with the book through the seasons, I see things come and go. Take caravans and campers for example, you see those in the spring, summer, and autumn, but not in the winter."

FINE ARTS

"Right in the middle of the illustration, I've put a big block of flats. In this way, I can show amusing things of the Dutch from close by. Because I also wanted to include paintings, I've given the top flat to a master forger. He has copied the famous Goldfinch by Fabritius from a postcard."

Carel Fabritius (1622-1654), *The Goldfinch* (1654)

George Breitner (1857-1923), *Girl in Red Kimono* (1893-1895)

Jan Cornelisz. Verspronck (1597-1662), *Portrait of a Girl in Blue* (1641)

Hans Holbein the Younger (ca. 1497-1543), *Desiderius Erasmus* (1523)

FIGURES FROM CHILDREN'S LITERATURE

Flip the Bear is a guest bear from television, created by writer Selma Noort (1960). Children can take the bear home with them for a night and learn how to care for him.

"Even though Pippi Longstocking is not Dutch, I've included her in the book for fun."

Pippi Longstocking is the main character in the series of Swedish children's books by Astrid Lindgren (1907-2002). The Dane Ingrid Vang Nyman (1916-1959) illustrated the very first edition, but many others have drawn Pippi in the 64 translations of the books.

MUSEUMS

The museum park has existed since 1927. There are no fewer than six museums: the Museum Boijmans Van Beuningen (visual arts from Holland and Europe, from the early middle ages to now), the Kunsthal (an exhibition hall presenting temporary and changing exhibitions), the Dutch Architecture Institute, the Natural History Museum, the museum house Villa Sonneveld, and the Chabot Museum (dedicated to painter and sculptor Hendrik Chabot (1894-1949).

In 1937, the Tax & Customs Museum was set up as an educational institution for future tax inspectors. In May 1940, the building went up in flames, but its founder Prof. Dr. J. van der Poel (1888-1982) managed to assemble another collection and the new museum was able to open its doors in 1948. The museum was completely renovated in 2012.

ARCHITECTURE

Architect Piet Blom (1934-1999) designed the Blaakse Bos (1982-1984) that is made up of thirty-eight cube houses, two super cubes and a block of flats, officially called the Blaak Tower, but commonly known as the "Pencil." The cube houses are on pillars that contain the stairway. There is a pedestrian area below them. The cube houses themselves have three storeys and the top floor has room for a small garden.

The first skyscraper in Rotterdam, the White House, dates from 1898 and is 141 feet tall. Architect Willem Molenbroek designed the eleven-storey building in Art Nouveau style.
The White House survived the bombing, but still shows the scars of shrapnel—a reminder of the battle for the Maas bridges in May 1940.

Francine Houben (1955), of the design agency Mecanoo, designed Montevideo, named after one of the warehouses that used to stand on this spot. When it was completed in 2005, it was 458 feet tall, making it the second tallest building in Holland and the highest block of residential flats.

"Here you can also see a piece of the modern library of Rotterdam. I thought it would be fun to fit it in somehow."

In 1983, the Central Library opened the doors of its new building designed by Jaap Bakema (1914-1981) and Hans Boot (1924). It is reminiscent of the Pompidou Centre in Paris. The building is sometimes called "the Glass Waterfall." The façade boasts a quotation by Erasmus: "The whole world is my fatherland."

The 610 foot tall Euromast is the highest observation tower in Holland. When the tower designed by Huig Aart Maaskant (1907-1977) was opened in 1960 by Princess Beatrix, it was only 331 feet tall; but in 1970 a space tower of 279 feet was placed on top of the existing Euromast. The visitors are taken to the highest point by a glass elevator.

"For the children, I've drawn the Tropicana swimming pool here in the corner."

The glass dome makes water paradise Tropicana (1988) on the Maasboulevard a real eye-catcher. It has, however, been empty since 2010 and in 2016 the building will be demolished to make way for houses for the elderly.

Hotel New York, also called "The Grand Old Lady," was opened in 1901. Three architects—Jan Muller (1874-1928), Constant Mari Droogleever Fortuin (1846-1928) and Christinus Bonifacius van der Tak (1872-1943)—designed the Art Nouveau building that, from 1901 to 1977 was the headquarters of the Holland-America Line. In 1993 it was converted into a hotel with an interior by the artist Dorine de Vos (1948).

WORDS

"When I walked through Rotterdam, I discovered that texts were everywhere. In the subway, on the garbage trucks, on the walls of buildings there are poems, texts, and quotations everywhere. I had to put it in the book since it is so unique to Rotterdam."

"Everything of value is helpless," is the text that in reality the building next to the Willem de Kooning Academy. It comes from the poem "The Very Old Sings" by the "Emperor of the Fifties" Lucebert (the pseudonym of Lubertus Jacobus Swaanswijk, 1924-1994).

FEYENOORD FOREVER

"These are Feyenoord shirts—two of them."

Feyenoord Rotterdam was founded in 1908 - although in the first few years it had three different names: Wilhelmina, H.F.C. and Celeritas. In 1924, it won the national championship for the first time. Since then, the club has enjoyed a leading place in Dutch top football. In 1970, Feyenoord was the first Dutch club to win the Europa Cup I.

NURSERY RHYME

Berend Botje went to sea
With his ship he sailed off free
The way was bent, the way was straight
Yet Berend Botje made them wait
One, two, three, four, five, six, seven
Is Berend Botje now in Heaven?
He's not here, he's not there
He's in America, that's where

A shipowner, Berend Drenth (1808-1893), nicknamed Berend Botje, sent his dilapidated ships out to sea. And then, when ship and crew were lost, he would pocket the insurance money. He is probably the Berend Botje in this nursery rhyme.

"We've done Rotterdam so now it's Amsterdam's turn. That's logical. Amsterdam has the Concertgebouw, the Amsterdam Theatre, the Bimhuis, organized music on the IJ, but that's not enough. Every summer they hold an evening concert on the water known as the Prinsengracht concert. The whole of the Prinsengracht [Prince's Canal] fills up with boats and people coming to listen. The tram still runs, clattering over the bridge, while music is performed.

For the concert, I painted a pianist and a full-figured singer. She bought her dress at the corner shop, but in a much larger size. The concert is held in the evening and that suited me just fine for in the evening everything white in the city is tinted yellow and orange. That's so beautiful!
I thought it would be nice to show the 17th century buildings of Amsterdam as a contrast to modern Rotterdam. Of course, both cities have old and modern buildings, but I had to make a choice. This is a fictitious canal because if I had chosen a real canal, I would have been forced to draw all the houses on it, and I wouldn't have been able to show half of Amsterdam. I didn't want that, so I made up a canal myself."

SECOND HALF OF AUGUST

AMSTERDAM

CANALS

C THE RING OF CANALS (1613-1662)
CITY EXPANSION IN THE 17TH CENTURY

At the end of the 16th century, Amsterdam was overrun with people who wanted to grab a share of the new prosperity. The city was bursting at the seams. A whole new city plan was devised and from 1613, the Herengracht (Lord's Canal), the Prinsengracht (Prince's Canal) and the Keizersgracht (Emperor's Canal) were dug. Fifty years later, the city centre looked the way it does now—houses for the rich on the canals, residential areas around it and wharves on the city outskirts.

"While I was strolling through the Historical Museum, I discovered that in the past there were a lot of horses in Amsterdam. Occasionally, one would fall into the canal so a type of crane was designed to hoist the horses out again."
J.C. Sinck designed the horse crane in 1860. The construction saved quite a few horses from the water. And Sinck took the horses that did not survive away—his father, Gerrit Sinck, was a horse butcher.

"They've got something in Amsterdam that doesn't exist anywhere else—a cat boat, where cats are given a good home. I really like cats, so the cat boat had to be in the book."
Since 1966, stray cats have been given a home on the cat boat in the Singel.

The best way to see Amsterdam is from the water. Various companies provide excursions through the canals, over the IJ, and through the harbor.

ORPHANS

Around 1520, the first Amsterdam orphanage, later the Burgerweeshuis (Civil Orphanage), was founded for the orphans of Amsterdam burghers, the official inhabitants of Amsterdam. The girls learned handwork and the boys were given training in a trade. Until 1919, the orphans from the Burgerweeshuis wore clothes that were bright red on the left and black on the right reflecting the colors of Amsterdam. Around that time, children whose parents were temporarily unable to care for them were also given a home. It was only in 1960 that the Burgerweeshuis relocated elsewhere, and in 1991 it ceased to exist as orphanage.

TOO LATE

"Every figure I paint is there for a reason. This little girl is too late for her lesson."

TAXI!

"You have taxis in all shapes and sizes in Amsterdam and not just cars, but also bikes and water vessels."

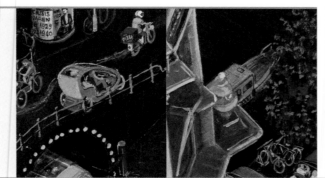

ON THE ROOF

"In Amsterdam, everybody makes a spot on their roof so that they can sit outside when it is hot."

THE JEWISH DISTRICT

"In the past, if you wanted to buy something on Sunday, you went to the Jewish District in Amsterdam because the shops were open there."

Since the 17th century, many Jews have come to Holland. They were not allowed to join the guilds and mainly became merchants or brokers. They settled in Amsterdam around the Waterlooplein, the Rapenburg, and the Jodenbreestraat. People still talk of this district as the Jewish District.

LOGO

 I AMSTERDAM is the logo that was presented in 2004 by the advertising agency KesselsKramer to give Amsterdam an international image.

BOOKS FOR CHILDREN

"The first children's bookshop in Holland was opened in Amsterdam by Rietje and Guillaume Nivard."

The "Kinderboekwinkel" (Children's Bookshop) opened in 1975 on the Rozengracht. Today, Holland has around thirty children's bookshops.

FAMOUS DUTCH

"You can discover a lot of history in Amsterdam, but one thing is cannot be missed—Anne Frank in the 'Achterhuis' [Secret Annex]. This is the rear of the Achterhuis, with a view of the tree that was the centre of controversy about whether or not a new one should be planted when the old tree died. I've drawn Anne with that small plaid diary in which she wrote."

C ANNE FRANK
(1929-1945)
PERSECUTION OF JEWS

Anne Frank was born to a Jewish family in Germany. Her family fled to Holland in 1933 because Hitler had come to power. Anne started keeping a diary at a young age, and, thanks to that, we know she really felt at home in Amsterdam. Her life changed when the Germans occupied the country. She had to go to an exclusively Jewish school, she had to wear a yellow star, and she wasn't allowed to go to the cinema or theatre. In 1942, the family went into hiding with four other people in the Achterhuis. Things went well for a long time, but after two years they were betrayed and arrested by the Germans. Anne died in a concentration camp, not long before the liberation in 1945.
She was one of the six million European Jews who did not survive the Second World War.

Rembrandt Harmenszoon van Rijn (c. 1606-1669) lived in this house between 1639 and 1658. It is now a museum and is completely furnished in the style of the 17th century.

C REMBRANDT
(c. 1606-1669)
THE GREAT PAINTERS

Rembrandt painted his most famous painting *The Company of Captain Frans Banning Cocq and Lieutenant Willem van Ruytenburgh Preparing to March Out* between 1640 and 1642; it has been known as *The Night Watch* since the 18th century. He probably painted it in a gallery off the courtyard of his house.
Although Rembrandt was a celebrated painter during his life, he often had no money. He bought more art than he could financially afford. He was declared bankrupt and the complete contents of his house were auctioned off.
When he died, a year after his only son Titus, his heirs had to rent a grave for him.

"There are two famous Huygens, father and son, Constantijn and Christiaan. Because the Huygens also provide a topic of history, I thought: I'll make a sign that says that the Constantijn Huygensstraat is closed. Then I can deal with the subject. But the topic of history turned out to refer to Christiaan and not Constantijn. Just my luck. Fortunately, the Amsterdam Science Park boasts the largest supercomputer in Holland and it is named after both Christiaan and Constantijn so it is the Huygens computer."

'This is the Rembrandt House complete with Rembrandt in the doorway. They have just— heaven knows how—carried out The Night Watch. In reality, the painting wouldn't go through the door, but these workmen have somehow managed to do it."

C ALETTA JACOBS
(1854-1929)
WOMEN'S EMANCIPATION

When Aletta Jacobs attended secondary school, girls were not allowed to study at university. She wanted to study so badly that she wrote a letter to the prime minister who wrote back to her father that Aletta could study at the university.
Aletta Jacobs not only ensured that women were granted access to higher education, she also distributed contraceptives and obtained better rights for shop girls (they were allowed to sit down occasionally). Together with other women who called themselves "feminists" and men, she fought for fifty years for women's rights. Women in Holland have been able to vote in political elections since 1919

C CHRISTIAAN HUYGENS (1629-1695)
SCIENCE IN THE GOLDEN AGE

Christiaan was the son of the famous poet Constantijn Hugens, who worked at the Dutch court. Thanks to this, Constantijn was able to obtain a good education. From an early age, Christiaan was interested in mathematics, physics, and astronomy. Throughout his life, he continued to study, carry out experiments, and make important discoveries. For example, he was the inventor of the pendulum clock, the principle of the steam engine, and the gunpowder motor. He also developed a telescope and used it to discover Titan, the first moon of the planet Saturn, as well as discovered the truth about the rings around Saturn.

PATRON SAINT

"The patron saint of Amsterdam is St. Nicholas. In reality, this plaque isn't in this spot, but on the corner of the Dam in a wall."

St. Nicholas is the patron saint of many trading and shipping cities. He is traditionally the protector of seafarers. Legend has it that he appeared to the sailors of a ship in distress. He took over the rudder and sailed the ship safely back to the harbor. In 1325, the Oude Kerk (Old Church) in Amsterdam was consecrated with St. Nicholas as patron saint. This was also where the Sinterklaas (the Dutch nickname for St. Nicholas) tradition began. After mass on December 6, the children were given money and small presents. It was the start of the annual festival which is still celebrated today.

PARTY!

"Everybody has to know when the Dutch hold a party. They hang flags and balloons outside, so that everybody can see there's something to celebrate."

YAWN

"In Holland, some drug stores boast a 'gaper' [yawner]."

Since the 17th century, "gapers" hang on the façades of chemists and drugstores. Generally they are Moors, and always have their mouths open to take their medicine.

DUTCH DESIGN

"Dutch design is also very indicative of Dutch culture and society. They are good at clean and austere. That's why I placed the Rietveld chair and other Dutch chair designs in the window."

From left to right:
- *Ruud Jan-Kokke (1965), Chair Spoinq*
- *Lounger Ferdinand white-red*
- *Gijs van der Sluis, Chair no. 50*
- *Gerrit Rietveld (1888-1964), Red-Blue Chair (ca. 1918-1923)*
- *Two of the famous steel tube chairs that Willem Hendrik Gispen (1890-1981) designed in the 1930s.*

⬛ DE STIJL (1917-1931)
REVOLUTION IN DESIGN

In 1917, Theo van Doesburg (1883-1931) founded the magazine *De Stijl* (*The Style*). With a group of artists including Piet Mondriaan and Gerrit Rietveld, Van Doesburg tried to reform art. His starting-point was to use as few colors as possible (red, blue, yellow, black, white and grey) and as little shape as possible (only straight lines and angles) to achieve the greatest possible harmony. Although the group existed for less than fifteen years, its influence on visual arts, design, and architecture was enormous.

SHOES AND DIAMONDS

Jan Jansen (1941) is one of the most famous shoe designers in Holland. He has four shops where his creations are sold.

"My great-grandfather was a diamond polisher."

Amsterdam is known as the city of diamond polishers. The first was entered into the national register in 1586. The special shape known as "Amsterdam Cut" is highly appreciated. The world-famous Koh-I-Noor diamond was cut and polished in Amsterdam.

GREEK HERO

In 1900, Football Club Ajax was founded. In 1908, the club won the Golden Cross, the prize for the best football club in Amsterdam. In 1918, it won its first national championship title. In 1969, Ajax was the first Dutch club to reach the final of the Europa Cup 1, but lost to AC Milan. That was put right in 1971 and in 1972 the club won its first World Cup. With thirty national titles to its name, Ajax is still playing at the top.
An Ajax shirt is white with a vertical red stripe.

FINE ARTS

"Mondriaan lived for some time in Amsterdam, but the painting he is working on here—one of his most famous— wasn't actually made in Amsterdam. A little poetic license is permissible, don't you think?"

Piet Mondriaan (1872-1944) is painting his *Composition with Red, Yellow and Blue*, dating from 1927, which he actually made in Paris. Mondriaan attended the National Academy for Fine Art in Amsterdam. He first attended the course for painters during the day and the drawing course in the evening. While still living in Holland, he concentrated mainly on painting landscapes. In 1911, he left for Paris after he had discovered cubism. Over the years, his work became increasingly abstract. His best-known works are *Broadway Boogie Woogie* and *Victory Boogie Woogie*, which he painted in New York.

"I had friends who thought I don't include enough music in my pictures. Holland does, of course, have some fantastic musicians. That's why I put the Concertgebouw Orchestra on a poster. In this way, I had the orchestra and the building in one go!"

The Concertgebouw (Concert Building), based on a design by Adolf van Gendt (1835-1901), took five years to build. The building that opened in 1888 has three halls. The Grote Zaal (Main Auditorium) was designed to allow late Romantic music to be heard at its best. Gustav Mahler conducted his own symphonies eleven times in this auditorium between 1903 and 1909.
The Concertgebouw Orchestra was founded in 1888. Since 1988 it may call itself the "Royal Concertgebouw Orchestra." It is considered one of the best symphony orchestras in the world.

"I really like ballet so a ballet academy had to be in the book. I also painted a panel for Hans van Manen and Rudi van Dantig, both of whom I love dearly."

Ballet dancer, choreographer, and photographer Hans van Manen (1932) worked for the National Ballet from 1973 to 1985. He created more than 120 ballets that are notable for their clarity and simplicity.
Choreographer and ballet dancer Rudi van Dantzig (1933-2012) was the house choreographer of the National Ballet from its foundation in 1961 and was artistic director from 1965 to 1991. His ballets—of which he created more than fifty—are frequently narrative and socially critical. His work included three ballets for the Russian ballet legend Rudolf Nureyev (1938-1993).

"The Cobra Museum in Amstelveen and the Stedelijk Museum in Amsterdam both have paintings by Karel Appel."

The work that is shown here is a mural without a title, which Karel Appel (1921-2006) painted in 1956 on the wall of the former restaurant of the Stedelijk Museum.
The Stedelijk Museum that opened in 1874 houses modern and contemporary art and reopened in 2012 after a renovation and rebuilding that lasted eight years.

Since 1977, the Uitmarkt (Out Market) in Amsterdam, in the last weekend in August, marks the opening of the cultural season. For three days, museums, theatres and other cultural groups present their new projects for the season ahead.

FIGURES FROM CHILDREN'S LITERATURE

"Minnie, from the book by Annie M.G. Schmidt, is walking on the roof. This picture is from the film that was made of the book, Minnie, with the kittens and the boy she falls in love with."

Annie M.G. Schmidt wrote *Minnie* in 1970. In 2001, the book was filmed with Carice van Houten in the role of Minnie.

ARCHITECTURE

The Westertoren is the tower of the Westerkerk (West Church). Although the church is owned by the Dutch Reformed Church, the tower is the property of the Municipality of Amsterdam.

The "Ouwe Wester" (Old Wester) is the tallest church tower in Amsterdam, measuring 275 feet high. For a century, from 1906 to 2006, the emperor's crown on the top was yellow, but now it has been restored to the original blue color from 1638.

A carillon hangs in the tower and sounds several times a day. It can also be played by hand.

*"Warehouses stand on the canal. I haven't depicted these as the modern houses they have now become, but as they were originally intended. In the 17th cen-*tury, they used to store goods brought here by the VOC. Here they are hoisting up a load."*

The majority of Dutch warehouses are in trading cities. The first warehouses date from around 1600. They are tall buildings, often narrow and deep, with a beam in the roof, which was used to hoist goods into the house. Most warehouses are on the water, ver which the goods could be transported.

"The palace on the Dam is a big building. If I were to show it normally, it would take up too much space, and as a child you won't really like that. Here it is shown on a poster. A bit crooked, but never mind."

The Royal Palace of Amsterdam is the reception palace of the Royal Family.

Originally, when it was built between 1648 and 1665, it was used as the city hall. It was designed by architect Jacob van Campen (1596-1657). It continued to fulfill this function until 1808, when it was given to the first king of the Netherlands, Louis Napoleon Bonaparte (1778-1846), as his palace. "Louis the Good"—the son of the famous Napoleon—was a much-loved king during the French occupation and he even championed the interests of Holland.

The palace is considered the most important monument in Holland from the Golden Age.

Theater Tuschinski, named after its founder Abraham Tuschinski (1886-1942), was opened in 1921 as a cinema with a large auditorium and a famous cabaret room, La Gaîté. The building, designed by Heyman de Jong (1882-1945) and completed by engineer D.C. Klaphaak, is a mix of Art Deco, Art Nouveau and the Amsterdam School.

Since then, the theatre has been enlarged and is now a cinema with six auditoriums. The Grote Zaal (Main Auditorium) has been restored to its former glory and hosts many international film premières.

Circus director Oscar Carré (1845-1911) opened Circus Carré on the Amstel in 1887. Circus performances were given in the winter months, and, from 1893, variety shows in the remaining months. After the lean years of the 1920s, Theater Carré, as it was by then known, became the home of Dutch revue, opera, and variety. It was also here that the first international musical was performed. Since 1987, the theatre may call itself the "Royal Theatre Carré."

This building by Michel de Klerk (1884-1923) and Piet Kramer (1881-1961) used to house the social democratic General Workers Cooperation "De Dageraad" (The Dawn). It is designed in the style of the Amsterdam School. The extensive use of brick, rounded shapes, and decorations in the façades is characteristic of this style from of modern architecture.

HISTORY

"Holland also had crisis years, but they can't be illustrated. How can you explain something like that without words? A poster provided the solution."

☐ THE CRISIS YEARS
(1929-1940)

SOCIETY IN DEPRESSION

The crisis that started in October 1929 in the United States soon spread to the rest of the world including Holland. In the years that followed, hundreds of thousands of people lost their jobs—one in four workers was out of a job for more than a year.

The unemployed were given a little help, enough for the rent and some food. They had to get a stamp twice a day to prove that they weren't working secretly on the side. They could also be required to accept compulsory work such as digging ditches, planting trees, or building dykes.

Although there were many complaints about the way the government handled things, little changed even after new elections. The big change did not come until after the Second World War.

"Making maps is also something typically Dutch. The famous Atlas Major by Blaeu was made in Amsterdam."

☐ THE ATLAS MAJOR
BY BLAEU (1662)

MAPPING THE WORLD

In the 17th century, when the Dutch were sailing round the world, both sailors and rich citizens were eager to obtain good world maps. Willem Janszoon Blaeu had himself retrained by a famous astronomer and, in 1605, opened a map printing shop. He compiled his land and sea maps based on existing maps and information from travel reports and stories told by seamen. His maps were very good for that time and soon became famous.

Willem's son Joan took over the business in 1638. His masterpiece was the *Atlas Major* from 1662 with no less than 600 maps and thousands of pages of information. The atlas was published in various languages and was extremely popular even though many of the maps it contained were already obsolete by then.

COAT OF ARMS

The coat of arms of Amsterdam consists of a red shield with a black vertical beam in which there are three white or silver crosses. It is sometimes said that the three crosses and the three colors stand for the three disasters that have hit Amsterdam: fire (red), water (white), and the plague (black). It is more probable that the coat of arms was adopted in the 13th century from the Persijn family. Knight Jan Persijn van Velsen (?-1283) was Lord of Amsterdam from 1280 to 1282. In other words, he owned the right to the "Manor of Amsterdam."

A LOT OF BIKES

"You can rent a bicycle in Amsterdam. Everybody will immediately see that you're on a tourist bike. And what do tourists do? They can't ride a bike and they always ride on the wrong side of the canal. Dutch might complain about them, but they really cannot do without tourists."

"In Amsterdam, you see bikes hanging over the railings along the canal or dangling from a lamp post. You will also see half-sunken boats that still have an old bike attached to a piece of rope."

LIBERAL AMSTERDAM

"There are ladies of pleasure in Amsterdam. I don't know whether people have already discovered it, but you can see one here—she is discreet, but she's there all the same, and a gentleman on a bike who just has to ride past her."

The Wallen (Embankment), or the Red Light District, named for the red lights behind the windows, is the best-known prostitute district in the western world. Prostitution has been going on here since at least the 15th century. There are both brothels and "women in the windows." Prostitution is legal in Holland if a prostitute is older than 21 and has entered her name in the "national register for prostitutes."

"On the bridge there is an electricity switch house with graffiti on it and, very tiny at the top right, a marijuana plant. Weed is Holland too, but please keep it quiet."

Cannabis, weed, or marijuana is illegal in Holland, but is tolerated. Anybody with less than five grams or who grows five plants will not, in principle, be prosecuted. It is not permitted to use drugs in the street, but the authorities turn a blind eye to its use at home or in a coffee shop (a weed shop). Every now and again, an attempt is made to restrict the sale of weed, but in the major cities, coffee shops are freely accessible to anybody above the age of eighteen.

"The very first marriage between persons of the same gender was held in Amsterdam. They can be proud of that.
Friends asked, 'What are you going to do in your book for the gay community?' I had first thought of a boat with gay men during the Gay Pride, but my friend said, 'Oh no, do me a favor!'
That's why I've shown same-sex marriage and there's music from a barrel organ."

The first marriage for people of the same sex was officially held in Holland on 1 April 2001. There is actually no such thing as a "same-sex marriage," because in Holland there is no legal difference between a marriage between a man and a woman and or between two men or two women.

DUTCH BLUES

"There are several nursery rhymes in this picture. One of them is 'To the Amsterdam Canals', played by an accordion player."

REFRAIN:
To the Amsterdam Canals
I have pledged my heart forever
Amsterdam fills my thoughts as the finest city in our land
All the Amsterdam people
All the lights in the evenings on the square
Nobody can wish for more
Than to be an Amsterdammer

(text: Pieter Goemans [1925-2000], 1949)

MODERN TRADITION

"I thought I should also paint squatters in Amsterdam. It may be illegal what they do, but they'll never stop and good for them."

Squatters take over an empty building and live there illegally. It is considered a protest against uninhabited housing and speculation in real estate. The first organized squatter actions took place in Holland in 1964. Since 2010, squatting has become illegal in Holland, but in many places it is tolerated because the squatter prohibition could contravene the constitution and officially court proceedings would have to be held before the squatters could be removed.

It is sometimes claimed that the graffiti culture came over to Europe from New York via Holland. Whatever the truth of the matter, graffiti began its rise to popularity in Holland in 1980 and is now a common phenomenon.

CITY LIFE — FIRST HALF OF SEPTEMBER

ARCHITECTURE

hands. That is why this floor had to be in the picture. By the way, there are family members of mine in this hospital."

"The mosque in the background is actually in Rotterdam."
The Essalam Mosque is, with its 160-foot high minarets, the largest mosque in Holland. It was opened in 2010 and the design is by the Dutch architect Wilfried van Winden (1955).

"The hospital here is a compilation of the teaching hospitals of Leiden and Amsterdam. It is wonderful that you can land on the top of a hospital in a helicopter. The top storey is the children's department. When I visit schools, I sometimes meet a child with a bald head and shaking

Architect Harry Reijnders (1954) designed Amsterdam Sloterdijk station that opened in 1986. The light design with a lot of steel and glass can be seen in other Dutch train stations as well.

"This soccer stadium does not exist. I made it up. If I had painted an existing stadium, I would have gotten into trouble with the supporters of the other soccer clubs."

PUBLIC TRANSPORT

"In this picture you can find all types of public transportation: train, subway, tram, and bus."

From left to right
– The logo of the Nederlandse Spoorwegen (Dutch Railways), designed in 1968 by Gert Dumbar (1940) and René van Raalte (1946).
– A subway sign—only Amsterdam and Rotterdam have subways. The stations can be recognized by the M.

– A tram symbol.
– The rear of a Connexxion bus. Connexxion was created in 1999 by merging a number of transportation companies. It handles regional passenger transport (including buses, taxis and ferry services) and ambulance care in a large part of Holland.

"In Holland you can rent a bike at the station and ride around for very little money. The one drawback is that the bikes are fitted with a coaster brake. I simply can't handle that kind of brake."
Since 2003, travelers at train and subway stations can rent a bike for the last part of their journey. People make use of this more than a million times a year.

HISTORY

"This is the monument to the abolition of slavery. Slavery is a dark stain on Dutch history. Although slaves never lived here, the Dutch used them as merchandise."
The *National Monument to Slavery* by Erwin de Vries (1929) was unveiled in 2002 in Amsterdam.

C SLAVERY (1637-1863)
TRADING IN PEOPLE AND FORCED LABOR IN THE NEW WORLD

Although no slaves were ever put to work in Holland, there was slavery in the Dutch colonies and Holland played a leading role in the slave trade. As early as 1528, there were merchants who shipped slaves from Africa to the Caribbean islands, but the real trade got started with the founding of the West Indies Company in 1621. It had previously been said that the slave trade was against Christian norms, but it was claimed that the Bible justified slavery in Genesis 9:25, "...Cursed be Canaan! The lowest of slaves will he be to his brothers." (NIV)
Around 1770, Holland traded no fewer than 6,000 people per year, but subsequently the numbers declined.
Holland did not abolish the slave trade until 1 July 1863, one of the last countries in the world to do so. By then, more than 500,000 people had been sold as slaves.

The Dutch slavery past is remembered every year on July 1.

"I could hardly show the Dutch Antilles—a group of islands— in Holland, so they had to appear on a poster. I have painted the picture everybody knows of the Antilles—the coast with the colored houses. Why does it appear on this spot? Because there happened to be a bus shelter here."
The colorful houses on the waterside are in Willemstad, the capital of Curaçao.

C SURINAM AND THE DUTCH ANTILLES
(from 1945)
DECOLONIZATION OF THE WEST

The islands of Aruba, Saba, St. Eustatius, Bonaire, St. Maarten, and Curaçao were claimed for Holland by the West Indies Company in 1634. From that moment, the Middle American archipelago was known by the name of the Dutch Antilles.
Several years later, Holland and England fought for each other's colonies in South and North America. In the Peace of Westminster in 1674, Holland relinquished Nieuw-Nederland (which became New York and part of the current United States) in exchange for Suriname.
In 1954, the Statute of the Kingdom of the Netherlands came into force, in which Suriname, the Dutch Antilles, and Holland became equal, and all inhabitants acquired the Dutch citizenship.
In 1975, Suriname became independent after paying compensation of 3.5 billion guilders. The Antilles and the Netherlands became two separate countries within the kingdom.
In 1986, Aruba obtained status seperate and became an independent country within the kingdom, with its own government and policy. In 2006, Curaçao and St. Maarten were also given the status separate. Saba, St. Eustatius and Bonaire were given the status of extraordinary municipality of Holland. With this, the Dutch Antilles ceased to exist.

"The First World War is also a topic of history. I think that very strange, for Holland was neutral in that period. Because no fighting took place here, I couldn't show any. I chose to adver-
tise the Army Museum in Delft. They have everything about the First World War there."
The Army Museum in Delft closed its doors in January 2013. In 2014, the National Military Museum will open in Soesterberg.

C THE FIRST WORLD WAR
(1914-1918)
WAR AND NEUTRALITY

In 1914, a world war broke out between Germany, Austria-Hungary, and the Ottoman Empire on the one side and the allies France, Belgium, and England on the other.
Even though Holland remained neutral, it came into contact with the war in all sorts of ways. The border with Belgium was cut off with a deadly electric fencing, yet many refugees managed to reach southern Holland.
Many Dutch merchants started profitable businesses with the Germans. In 1918, England impounded the Dutch merchant ships because Holland was thought to be helping the Germans.
Because supply ships were torpedoed and much less trade could take place with foreign countries, a food shortage arose. In 1917 and 1918, desperate housewives plundered the central food stores in Amsterdam and Rotterdam because their families were starving.
In 1918, when the allies gained the upper hand, the German Kaiser Wilhelm II requested asylum in Holland. It was granted, much against the wishes of the allies. Wilhelm II lived in Holland until his death in 1941.

JOHAN CRUIJFF

Johan (Hendrik Johannes) Cruijff (1947) is perhaps the most famous Dutch soccer player ever. He was elected European Soccer Player of the 20th century and ended up in second place for the election of World Soccer Player of the Century. After his soccer career, he became a trainer, coaching Ajax and FC Barcelona, where he was known as *El Salvador,* the Savior. He has also founded a number of institutions for sport and marketing and founded the Johan Cruyff Foundation, which is dedicated to encouraging disabled children and young people to participate in sport.

FLOWERS

"Here I have drawn a flower shop, because it's typically Dutch to take flowers, chocolates, or fruit with you when you go to visit somebody in the hospital."

HOOLIGANS

"In the background near the stadium you see fighting fathers. I made them with my heart in France, in the styles they fight in the strips of Asterix and Obelix. They bash each other out of their shoes. I like to exaggerate things. The Mobiele Eenheid (Mobile Unit) naturally turn up."

SPECIAL BRIGADE

In 1934, there was a big demonstration in Amsterdam by the unemployed against the lowering of benefits, and it got out of hand. Known as the Jordaan uprising, it was clear that the police were incapable of controlling such riots. That led to the setting up of the Karabijnbrigade (Carbine Brigade) for specially trained agents. In the years 1970 and 1980, the time of the squatter riots, the Mobiele Eenheid (ME) quickly became more professional. Today there are more than forty platoons, each with 45 specially trained policemen who often in turn form specialized units within the ME.

YUCKY!

"Dog poop on the pavement is a plague in every city in Holland."

DUTCH SPECIALTIES

"Somebody asked me: 'Charlotte, have you thought of Libelle and Margriet?' I hadn't, so I quickly painted a poster. Initially, an advertisement for C&A hung here, but that could be removed, because C&A appears later in the book."
Libelle (Dragonfly) and Margriet (Daisy) are the two oldest women's magazines of Holland. Libelle has existed since 1934, Margriet since 1938. In content, there is little difference between the magazines. They both contain articles about housekeeping, society, and lifestyle plus columns and stories.

In 1896, Jacob Blokker and his wife opened "The cheap iron and wood shop." It grew quickly, and four sons started a chain under the name Blokker Brothers in the 1930s. Today there are more than 800 shops with the name Blokker, primarily in Holland and Belgium.

"In the park, there is a pram designed by a Dutch designer."

In 1994, design student Max Barenburg graduated with honors with the design for a baby buggy. No pram manufacturer was interested, so in 1999, Barenburg started his own company with his brother-in-law. The Bugaboo was an instant success and when, in 2002, the Bugaboo Frog appeared in the television series *Sex and the City*, there was no stopping it. Everybody wanted a Bugaboo.

In 1938, Simon Loos began a messenger service between Hoorn and Alkmaar. In 1960, the company won an order for shop distribution. Today, transport and logistics company Simon Loos has 400 trailer trucks that operate mainly in Benelux but also farther afield.

"When I had finished the book and had drawn TNT in it, the company was suddenly renamed PostNL. I left it the way it was because it is part of history."
In 1799, the State was responsible for handling the mail in Holland. Later, telephone service was added, and in 1928 this resulted in the Staatsbedrijf der Posterijen, Telegrafie en Telefonie (PTT—State Company for Post, Telegraphy and Telephony). In 1989, the PTT was made independent. In 2002, the name PTT Post was changed to TPG Post, which, through mergers,

became in 2006 TNT Post and finally, in 2011, PostNL.

"Here is an employee of KLM in her uniform. She's going to Schiphol by train."
In 2010, the flight attendants of KLM got new uniforms designed by couturier Mart Visser (1968). The base color is KLM-blue—as it has been since 1971—with an orange accent referencing the Royal Family (Van Oranje-Nassau). The flight attendants can chose pants, a pencil skirt, or a wider skirt.

Holland occupies fifth place on the list of European dairy producers. For generations, milk and associated products have been actively marketed with slogans such as "Milk. The white engine" and promotional figures such as Joris Driepinter (drinks three pints of milk a day).
Today, there is considerable discussion about the allegation that "milk is good for everybody." The Dutch still eat and drink an average of 68 gallons of dairy products per year.

"When I was working on the book, the Holdorp and Hin boys were working in my house. That's why they are here."
Marco Holdorp and Michel Hin have been working together in their own carpentry and maintenance company since 2006.

MUSICIANS

"Here an orchestra is preparing to go on tour. Some come from the station, others from the subway and others from the tram. What is so great about musicians? They carry cases in the same shape as their instrument."

"In front of the station, three Romanians are singing sad songs to collect money."
As long as artists do not perform with more than three people together and do not perform for longer than thirty minutes continuously, they can perform on the street without a permit.

NURSERY SCHOOL AND SWIM CLASS

"In Holland, some nursery schools don't have yards. The children in such a nursery are placed in a large wooden box on wheels and they go off to the park with their caregiver so that they get out in the fresh air."

"All Dutch children can swim. Here there is an ugly swimming pool where they have just obtained their A diploma."
Swimming diplomas have been given out in Holland since 1892. Today there is Swimming ABC, a series of three diplomas that prepare swimmers for swimming in open water and what they should do if they unexpectedly find themselves in water.

EVERYTHING IS ORGANISED

"Something typical for Holland are separate bicycle routes and the enormous number of directional signs on the road so that you can never end up on the wrong side of the road or make a mistake about right of way and so on. It has all been thought through to the tiniest detail."
Anybody who obtains his driving license in Holland has to find his way through 24 types of white and yellow lines on the road surface. There are also blue stripes where you use a parking disc indicating the time you parked your car, and green stripes where you mustn't drive faster than 60 mph.

"The waste collection in Holland is well organized. Here you see a truck that collects household waste that has been placed beside the road. Somewhere else I've drawn waste containers in which people can place their separated trash."
The Dutch produce around 1,100 pounds of waste per person each year, of which more than 85% is food or food packaging. Thanks to an ingenious waste collection separation and recycling system, today more than 80% of the waste is reused.

"This is something else I like: letterboxes on two levels. If you are small or handicapped, or drive around on a mobility scooter, you can't reach the top one."

"The Dutch think they should provide help to all sorts of

people. For the blind people, they make a path for crossing the road, which can be felt with their stick."
Blind routes are being constructed in a growing number of places in Holland. A corrugated edge to the tile helps the blind find the right way through the city. Metal audio tiles indicate an intersection and special ticking traffic lights make it clear when it is safe to cross.

"They've even thought up something for a handicapped dog. A dog can live longer with a wheeled cart."

WHIR-ER WHIR-ER

"My other half works in Leiden not far from the teaching hospital. He sometimes hears the screeching tires of the ambulance through his window. He and some colleagues once had a nasty experience when they were using a crosswalk during their break and they were nearly run over by an ambulance. They com-

plained, which is a very Dutch thing to do."
An ambulance has reflecting red and blue diagonal strips on a yellow background.

MONEY

The first Dutch Grenswisselkantoor (GWK—Border Exchange Office) opened in 1927. In 2004, the international company Travelex acquired the GWK banks.

VIRGIN

The entrance to the park is the same as that of the Vondel Park in Amsterdam. On the pillar sits the *Amsterdam City Virgin* (1883), the personification of the city of Amsterdam, made by the sculptor Friedrich Schierholz (1840-1894). The virgin is holding a shield of the city of Amsterdam in one hand and with her other is inviting people to enter the park.

NURSERY RHYME

One two three four, hat of, hat of
One two three four, hat of paper
If you haven't got a hat
Make one of cardboard
One two three four, hat of paper
One two three four, hat of, hat of
One two three four, hat of paper
If the hat doesn't fit
Put it in the glass cabinet
One two three four, hat of paper

The rhyme dates from 1830 and is written to the tune of a military drum march. At that time, the Belgian Revolution was raging and the Southern Netherlands had declared their independence. The Dutch government sent in the army, but there were too few uniforms for the conscripts. The country soldiers were therefore given a hat made of parchment-like paper.

TRADITIONS AND FESTIVALS

"When Oranje plays soccer, the people decorate their houses with orange flags, balloons, garlands and so on."
The Dutch soccer team played its first match in 1908. It would take eighty years—until 1988—before it won its only international championship, the European Championship.
The team is nicknamed Oranje (Orange), after the color of the shirts and the name of the Royal Family (Van Oranje-Nassau). When Oranje plays, the whole of Holland turns orange.

Since the 17th century, the rich of Holland would eat rusks with muisjes ("mice"—aniseed seeds with a sugar coating) at the birth of a child. Poorer people offered white bread with sugar.
The aniseed was supposed to be good for breast-feeding, for the recovery of the womb, and was supposed to ward off evil.
Traditionally, the muisjes are pink and white. Since the birth of Princess Beatrix in 1938, orange muisjes are eaten when a child is born to the Royal Family. In the middle of the 1990s, special blue and white muisjes appeared on the market to celebrate the birth of a boy.

"The third Tuesday in September, Prinsjesdag (Little Prince's Day), is a special day in The Hague. The king and queen and their court ride from the palace to the Binnenhof. The government of Holland sits in The Hague, so I thought this illustration should be somewhat more formal that the previous one. The Hague is also where you find Madurodam, which proved to be my salvation. I really wanted to do something with all the big famous buildings in Holland. The miniature city was my chance to put them in the book.

Tiny little figures stand among the houses in Madurodam. The one time I went there, I remember thinking it would be fun if they came to life. While that can't happen in real life, I can draw it! The children in the illustration see the cars drive around but not the grownups. If you look closely, you'll see that only one child is looking at a building, the rest are looking at other things. A teacher who has studied hard to be able to explain all this is standing there talking while the pupils are fighting, arguing, gossiping—doing all the things that you do in a class except paying attention. As an extra, I've put Fingerling into the picture with fifteen of his friends. All fifteen of them have hidden themselves, but you can find them if you look hard enough."

THE HAGUE ON PRINSJESDAG

On Prinsjesdag, the king gives the "speech from the throne." In the speech, he talks about everything that has gone on during the past year and also gives a preview of the plans and measures that the government have in mind for the coming year.

SECOND HALF OF SEPTEMBER

HOLLAND AND INDONESIA

C INDONESIË (1945-1949)
A REPUBLIC FIGHTS TO FREE ITSELF

At the end of the 16th century and for a large part of the 17th century, the Republic of the Netherlands conquered— often in a violent, bloody way—a large part of the Malay Archipelago, which later became known as "Dutch East Indies."

During the Second World War, on 8 March 1942, the Dutch East Indies fell into the hands of Japan. In the period that followed, Indonesian nationalist Sukarno (1901-1970) worked with the Japanese against the Dutch. On 7 August 1945, two days after Japan had surrendered, Sukarno declared Indonesian independence.

For four years, Holland resisted independence, with two peaks in violence, the so-called "police actions." The result was 5,000 dead on the side of the Dutch and 150,000 among the Indonesians. Finally, in December 1949, Holland recognized the independence of Indonesia and the presidency of Sukarno.

"The Hague remains the symbol of the government, as well as what were formerly the colonies. That is the reason that Hotel Des Indes is included here."

Hotel Des Indes (the hotel of the Indies), opened in 1881, is one of the oldest and most prestigious hotels in The Hague. It offers lodging to kings, emperors, statesmen, artists, scholars, and old Indonesia visitors. The building dates from 1858, when it was built as city palace for baron van Brienen van de Groote Lindt (1814-1863), personal advisor to King Willem II. After his death it was sold.

"In the past, the people who worked in the colonies often spent their leave in The Hague. That's why you have a lot of this type of shop with colonial wares and delicacies."

ROYAL AIRLINE

The Koninklijke Luchtvaart Maatschappij voor Nederland en Koloniën (KLM— Royal Airline Company for Holland and Colonies) was founded in 1919. From its first flight in 1920, Schiphol Airport has been the home base of KLM. In 2004, KLM merged with Air France and became Air France-KLM. Subsidiaries of KLM include Martinair and Transavia.

ARCHITECTURE

The Castalia with its 340-foot high towers stands out above the skyline of The Hague. The building, completed in 1998, was designed by the American architect Michael Graves (1934) and houses the Ministry of Heath, Welfare, and Sport. The pointed roofs have earned it the nickname of "the Hague Tits."

"This is the Koppelpoort ("connection gate") Amersfoort. The city has a genuine medieval inner city. It is beautiful and well worth a visit."
More than 10,000 years before Christ, the first people in the area lived around Amersfoort. The current medieval city centre dates from the 14th and 15th centuries. The city walls were built between 1380 and 1450. After a number of miracles involving a statue of Mary (in a single century, no less than 542 miracles were recorded), Amersfoort became a favored place of pilgrimage.

"The townhall of Hilversum was made by Dudok, and my grandfather worked on it with him. That is why I chose the city hall in Hilversum rather than the Gemeente Museum (Municipality Museum) in The Hague, designed by Berlage. The two buildings look like each other,

although you're not supposed to say that."
Willem Marinus Dudok (1884-1974) designed the Raadhuis (City Hall) of Hilversum, which was built between 1928 and 1931. This building is considered the most important work by Dudok.

"This is the oldest train station in Holland."
Station Valkenburg opened in 1853. The building is made of marl blocks and was designed by Jacobus Enschedé.

"The staff of Madurodam is just moving the Dam."
The National Monument (1956) on the Dam in Amsterdam was designed by Jacobus Johannes Pieter Oud (1890-1963) in remembrance of the World War II. It contains reliefs by Paul Grégoire (1915-1988) and sculptures by Johannes Anton Rädecker (1885-1956). There are two stone lions by Jan Willem Rädecker (1924-2009), who completed the work of his father after his death. Twelve urns stand in the curved wall. They contain earth from military cemeteries and places where Dutch men and women faced the firing squad—one from each Dutch province at the time and one from the former Dutch East Indies. Every year, the monarch lays a wreath at the monument on May 4, the National Remembrance Day for the Dead.

The Ridderzaal in the Binnenhof was commissioned by Count Willem II and built between 1248 and 1280. As the years passed, other buildings were constructed around it and for centuries these have formed the heart of Dutch politics.
The Hague has been built around the Binnenhof.

In 1254, work started on building the cathedral of the bishopric of Utrecht. A lack of funds meant it was never completed and the nave was nothing more than a wooden roof. Until 1559, the Dom Church remained Holland's only cathedral. In 1674, a tornado destroyed the church's nave. The debris was not cleared away until 1826, and then the Dom Square was formed between the Dom Tower and the Dom Church.
With its 368 feet, the Dom Tower is the tallest church tower in Holland.

The Rotterdam architect Pieter Adams (1778-1846) designed the characteristic Winkel van Sinkel (Shop of Sinkel) on the Oudegracht in Utrecht. The façade is decorated with pillars in the shape of women known as *caryatids*.
The shop of Anton Sinkel (1785-1848) opened in 1839 and had a famous advertising slogan:

**Everything's for sale
You can get**

**Baskets with figs
Boxes of pomade
Bottles of pop
Heads and caps
And ladies corsets
Sweets for chewing
And pills for pooping**

The shop closed its doors in 1921. Today the building houses a restaurant and also hosts cultural events.

The Rietveld Schröder House (1925), designed by Gerrit Rietveld (1888-1964) for Truus Schröder-Schräder (1889-1985) in line with the ideas of De Stijl (see p. 18), is on the UNESCO World Heritage list. Schröder and Rietveld worked closely together on the design and became lovers. When Rietveld's wife died, Rietveld moved in with Schröder.

The construction of the Cathedral Basilica of St. John the Evangelist in 's-Hertogenbosch began around 1370 on the spot where a Romanesque church had stood. The new Gothic church was built partly over the old church. The building was completed around 1530 and consecrated as cathedral in 1559. It is considered the high point of Brabant Gothic. Around 600 sculptures are used both inside and outside of the cathedral.
In 1929, the cathedral was given the honorary title of "basilica."

Den Bosch has fifty globe houses, built in 1984 from a design in the 1970s by architect Dries Kreijkamp (1937). The globes are on a pillar and look like toadstools with a round hat. The houses are suitable for one or two residents and are sometimes called "Bossche bollen" (Bosch Balls—the name of a local cake).

The International Court of Justice of the United Nations is housed in the Peace Palace. During The Hague Peace Conference in 1899, the decision was made that a Permanent Court of Arbitration—a mediation court for international disputes—should arise on that spot. The choice fell on a design by the French architect Louis Cordonnier (1854-1940), who adapted it and implemented it in collaboration with the Dutch engineer Johan van der Steur (1865-1945). The palace, which opened in 1913, contains a library for international law and the Hague Academy for International Law.

Philips, the lighting and electronics company, had the Evoluon built in 1966 as a gift to the city of Eindhoven. Louis Kalff (1897-1976) and Leo de Bever (1930) designed the technology museum in the shape of a flying saucer that seems to be hovering above the ground. In 1989, the museum was closed, and the building is now used as a congress and event center.

The Maeslant Barrier, built between 1991 and 1997, is part of the Delta Works. It consists of two enormous walls that can shut off the Nieuwe Waterweg (New Waterway) if there is a threat of high tide water. The barrier works completely automatically, but if the technology should go wrong, it can still be operated by hand.

CLASSY

"There are some very posh people living in The Hague, who wear nice coats and high-heeled shoes. You also have Haagse Harry."

In The Hague, there is a big distinction between Hagenars—the posh people—and Hagenese, the common people of the city. Haagse Harry is a cartoon figure who appeared in the early 1990s and speaks the common dialect of The Hague. Haagse Harry was created by the cartoonist Marnix Rueb (1950).

MUSEUM

"I've drawn for the Children's Book Museum, so I had to include it."

The Children's Book Museum opened in 1994, as part of the Literary Museum. It featured a review of the history of children's literature and it also held exhibitions. From 2007 to 2010, the museum was rebuilt as an interactive multimedia discovery world.

FAST TRAIN

"Madurodam has a commuter train and also a high-speed train, and they do run—contrary to what usually happens in Holland."

FAMOUS DUTCH

"Spinoza died in The Hague so that is why I've shown him here."

[C] SPINOZA (1632-1677)
IN SEARCH OF TRUTH

Baruch Spinoza was the son of Sephardic Jews who had fled from Portugal. He was very interested in philosophy and theology and wrote articles in which he claimed that Jews were not the Chosen People and that the Bible was not inspired by God but written by prophets. He was expelled from the Jewish community because of his writings and activities.

To earn money, Spinoza ground lenses for spectacles and microscopes and continued with his study at the same time. In his most important work, *Ethica Ordine Geometrioa Demonstrata*, he claimed that God did not stand above people, but that everything is God, including mankind itself. People should live an independent, calm, and reasonable life in order to discover that.

Spinoza died at a young age from a lung disease, probably caused by the lens dust he had breathed in for years. The *Ethica* appeared in the year after his death and generated much protest. As a result, the books of Spinoza were forbidden in Europe for 200 years.

[C] FLORIS V (1254-1296)
A DUTCH COUNT AND
DISSATISFIED NOBLES

Floris V was two years old when Frisians murdered his father and he inherited the title of "Count of Holland and Zeeland."

He reached his majority and formally became the count on his twelfth birthday.

Over time, he added West Friesland and a part of the bishopric of Utrecht to his county.

The lands of Floris were so large that he was assisted by a number of nobles, but they were not in favor of him because

Floris was good for the farmers. His nickname was "der keerlen God," the god of the farmers. The nobles were no longer allowed, much to their displeasure, to suppress the farmers.

When Floris negotiated a treaty with the king of France in order to fight the Count of Flanders, the nobles decided to intervene. They imprisoned Floris in his own castle, the Muiderslot, which he had had built in 1280.

The farmers started an uprising to free their Floris. When the nobles tried to smuggle Floris out of the castle, they ran into an ambush of farmers. At that moment, they decided that Floris must never be delivered into the hands of the farmers while still alive and they stabbed him to death.

[C] WILLIBRORD (658-739)
SPREAD OF
CHRISTIANITY

The English Willibrord was ordained as priest in Ireland when he decided to dedicate his life to converting heathens. In 690, he left with a number of disciples for the Frisian kingdom that, at the time, covered the whole of modern Holland and part of the German North Sea coast. Utrecht was the most important city. Willibrord adopted a clever approach. To protect himself, he sought the support of the Frankish major-domo (the Franks and the Frisians were arch enemies) and had himself ordained by the Pope as archbishop of the Frisians. He was given a Roman fort in the centre of Utrecht as his seat. Initially, he supervised his missionary work from an abbey he had built himself in Echternach (Luxembourg), but when the Franks had driven the Frisians out of Utrecht, he went to live in his fort.

Willibrord achieved great success. At the end of his life, the majority of the Frisians on the Dutch coast had converted to Christianity.

DUTCH SPECIALTIES

One evening, baron Hendrik Hop (1723-1808) from The Hague, left his cup of coffee with sugar sitting on the stove. He so liked the coffee caramel that was in his cup the next morning that, when his doctor told him that he must no longer drink coffee, he visited the 'confectionery shop' he lived above and asked whether they could make this sort of caramel for him.

The shop also started selling the resulting sweets, which became known as "the morsels of baron Hop." In 1880, the name was changed to "Haagsche hopjes."

 A "Bossche bol" is also called a chocolate ball. It is a large éclair, with a diameter of nearly five inches, filled with whipped cream and coated with melted plain chocolate. The baker Henri van der Zijde in Den Bosch sold such a cake for the first time in 1920. When the delicacy was also sold outside the city limits, the name "Bossche bol" became popular.

"In common with all museums, Madurodam also has a café-restaurant. There, you can eat poffertjes, a typical Dutch dish."

"Poffertjes" were already appearing in Dutch cookery books halfway through the 18th century. They were also known as bollebuisjes (bunchy tubes) or broedertjes (little brothers). They are mini pancakes cooked on a baking tray or pan filled with dents. The batter contains yeast, which makes them rise in the pan. The poor people's version was made of buckwheat, water, and yeast. The rich added wheat flour, milk, and eggs. Poffertjes are still a favorite dish and are best served with butter and castor sugar.

DAUGHTER

"Here is my daughter. She's attending the art academy in The Hague."

FINE ARTS

Johannes Vermeer (1632-1675), *Girl With the Pearl Earring* (1665-1667)

"The Hague is also the home of the Mauritshuis where a very famous painting by Vermeer hangs, Girl With the Pearl Earring."

The Mauritshuis, a city palace from the 17th century that now serves as a museum, houses a collection of 800 paintings, mainly from the Golden Age (the 17th century) and several major paintings from the 18th century.

THE KINGS DRIVE

"A drive by the king takes place according to an elaborate protocol including security, coachmen, and lackeys. The lackeys are in blue and the coachmen in red."

The drive begins at Noordeinde Palace and ends at the Ridderzaal (Knights' Hall) in the Binnenhof. The king and queen sit in the Golden Carriage, a gift from the people of Amsterdam to Queen Wilhelmina in 1898. The carriage is made of teak and gold leaf. Only when the Head of State is seated in the carriage are there eight horses in harness, otherwise there are only six.
Four lackeys walk on either side of the carriage. They open the doors and lower the steps to make getting in and out easier.

"The Binnenhof in The Hague doesn't fit in the picture, but fortunately it is also in Madurodam. Here, the king and queen arrive at the Ridderzaal. Tiny, but they get there."

"Crowds of older people come to see the ride in wheelchairs and completely packed in plastic, for the staff don't take any risks."

They wear orange hats on their heads and hold flags in their hands to wave as the king passes."

Since the middle 1990s, nearly all female ministers wear a hat on Prinsjesdag (Little Prince's Day). They can simply be a nice piece of headwear, but increasingly the hats make a political statement.

FIGURES FROM CHILDREN'S LITERATURE

books appeared about the Wicked Witch, all of which were illustrated by Annemarie van Haeringen (1959). A selection of the stories was filmed for television.

Fingerling is a tiny man, the size of your pinkie finger, from the similarly named books by Dick Laan (1894-1973). *The Adventures of Fingerling* first appeared in 1939, and since then 29 books and 211 stories have been published. There has also been a film with Fingerling in the main role.

"This is a princess by Gertie Jaquet, a friend from my class."
Gertie Jacquet (1958) drew and wrote *The Little Sweet Princess* (2009).

"This is the Wicked Witch of Hanna Kraan. Hanna died when I was making this illustration. Now, she's standing here forever."
Hanna Kraan (1946-2011) made her début in 1990 with *Tales of the Wicked Witch*. Six

"Fien by Sanne te Loo is standing in front of the hat shop. Her story is about a queen and her beautiful hats, something for which Queen Beatrix was famous, so that fits in nicely here."
Sanne te Loo (1972) drew and wrote *Simply Fien* (2007).

HISTORY

C EUROPE (from 1945)
DUTCH AND EUROPEANS
In 1951, Holland, Luxembourg, France, Germany, Belgium and Italy signed the Treaty of Paris about coal and steel collaboration. Six years later, these same countries formed the EEC, the European Economic Community, which regulated free trade in products between these countries. More and more countries joined the community.

In 1993, signing the Treaty of Maastricht, which included the decision to form an Economic and Monetary Union with one European currency, the euro, sealed the collaboration between what had by then become twelve EEC countries. Collaboration in justice would also be undertaken.
In 2007, the Treaty of Lisbon was signed that meant that the European Union with its own European Constitution became a fact. The treaty was signed by 27 countries and came into operation on 1 December 2009.

"Here, the first Dutch aircraft is flying around. It was called the Spin [Spider]. It took off in my city, in Haarlem."
Anton Herman Gerard (Anthony) Fokker (1890-1939) built the Fokker Spin in 1910. But before he could try it out himself, his business partner flew it into a tree. Fokker taught himself to fly in the second Spin, but again his business partner crashed the plane. Fokker finally flew round the tower of the St. Bavo Church in Haarlem in Spin 3 on 13 August 1911. A total of 22 Spins followed.

NURSERY RHYMES

"In front of the oldest station of Holland there are seven little cars from a very well known song."

On a little station
Early in the morning
Stood seven cars
Neatly in a row
And the engine driver
Turned on the wheel
Hakke hakke puff, puff
Away we go!

In The Hague lives a count
And his son's named Jantje
If you ask where your dad lives
He points with his hand
With his finger and his thumb
In his hat he wears a feather
On his arm a basket
Bye bye, my dear Jantje

It could be that the Jantje in the rhyme is Jan I, the son of Count Floris V, who lived in The Hague. Jan, however, is a very common Dutch name.
The sculpture *Jantje of The Hague* was made in 1976 by Ivo Coljé (1951-2012). Jantje has toadstools in his basket.

THE VELUWE FIRST HALF OF OCTOBER

HISTORY

ⒸTHE STATE BIBLE (1637)
THE BOOK OF BOOKS

Until the beginning of the 17th century, various Dutch translations of the Bible were in use. These were translations of translations.

During the Synod of Dordrecht—the national meeting of the reformed church in 1618-1619—it was decided to make a new translation of the Bible directly from the original languages of Hebrew, Aramaic, and Greek.

The States-General agreed in 1626 to pay for the translation, and in 1635 it was ready. It was approved in 1637 by the States-General. 500,000 copies were printed in the following twenty years.

The use of the vernacular language in the translation laid the foundation for Standard Dutch, and many sayings from the State Translation are still in common use.

In 2010, the Revised State Translation was revised into present-day Dutch.

On 3 October 1574, the Spanish siege of Leiden came to an end. It had lasted for many months and famine raged in Leiden.

The Prince of Orange decided to drive away the Spanish by breaching the dykes and flooding the land around Leiden. In the night and morning of 2/3 October, the water rose and the Spanish did indeed flee. There is a story of a little boy, Cornelis Joppensz, who entered the Spanish camp and discovered that the Spaniards had left in such a hurry that a stew was left waiting to be served.

On the morning of 3 October, the Sea Beggars—the accomplices of Willem of Orange—sailed to the city with herring and white bread to feed the population and relieve Leiden.

Every year, the people of Leiden celebrate the relief with a major festival, with free white bread, herring and stew.

ROYAL PALACE THE LOO

Palace "Het Loo" was commissioned by Stadtholder Willem III (1650-1702), who later became King of England. Jacobus Roman (1640-1716) designed the classical building that has been extended in the course of time. Until 1975, the palace was the summer residence of stadtholders and heads of state. After it was restored to how it had been in the 17th century, it was opened in 1984 as national museum.

"This is the small caravan of Queen Wilhelmina. She didn't live in it, but painted in it."
Queen Wilhelmina (1880-1962) was a rather good amateur artist. She left behind more than a thousand paintings, sketches and drawings.

WHITE BICYCLES

There are 1700 white bicycles in the Hoge Veluwe National Park which may be used free of charge in the park. The total area of the park more than 20 square miles.

TRADITIONS AND FESTIVALS

"The start of October is very important for those of us who illustrate and write children's books because that is when Children's Book Week is held. There's a nice long children's book truck here filled with books."
The annual Children's Book Week—which used to last eight days and has now been extended to ten days—was first held in 1955 and puts the Dutch children's book in the spotlight. Since 1962, there have been activities around a certain theme. There's a national book market, an inexpensive picture book is made available and, when people spend a certain amount on children's books, they are given a free copy of the Children's Book Week Present written by one of the many Dutch children's book authors.

"In Holland, October 4 is Animal Day. Here activists are demonstrating against hunting. The Dutch like demonstrating and they always sing when they're doing it."
In 1929 a decision was made to hold World Animal Day on October 4, the feast day of St. Francis of Assisi. In Holland, they have celebrated Animal Day since 1930.

FINE ARTS

"The Kröller-Müller is a wonderful museum in Holland. It houses various styles of art and features beautiful sculptures in the garden."

Helene Kröller-Müller (1869-1939) collected nearly 11,500 art objects, primarily from the 19th and 20th century. In 1938 she achieved her dream of creating a museum house. She died just a year later. Over the years, the Kröller-Müller Museum has expanded. There is now more modern sculpture and the sculpture garden is one of the largest in Europe.

"In my opinion, Vincent van Gogh—an important painter for the Dutch—produced his best work when he was living abroad, yet I really wanted to show his work. I have made an announcement for the Kröller-Müller Museum with a painting by Van Gogh, a copy of which hung in the hallway of my grandparent, a café by night in Arles."

Vincent van Gogh (1853-1890), *Café Terrace at Night* or *Terrasse du café le soir, Place du forum, Arles* (1888)

Oswald Wenckebach (1895-1962), *Monsieur Jacques* (1956)

Barbara Hepworth (1903-1975), *Squares with Two Circles* (1964)

Claes Oldenburg (1929), *Trowel* (1971)

Jean Dubuffet (1901-1985), *Jardin d'Email* (1973)

FIGURE FROM CHILDREN'S LITERATURE

Kikker (Frog) is the main character in more than twenty picture books by Max Velthuijs (1923-2005). The stories of Frog have won the most prestigious Dutch prizes and appear in more than fifty languages.

ARCHITECTURE

"This is Sint-Hubertus, the house where the Kröller-Müller family spent the last years of their lives together."

Hendrik Petrus Berlage (1856-1934) designed the Sint Hubertus country lodge in 1914 as a country house for Anton Kröller (1862-1941) and Helene Kröller-Müller (1869-1939). The construction took five years from 1915 to 1920, mainly because the clients constantly interfered with the building and its design. Berlage resigned when the Kröller-Müllers wanted to build a conservatory of which he could not approve. The Flemish artist-architect Henry Van de Velde (1863-1957) completed the work.

A traditional Veluwe farmhouse under a thatched wolf roof includes a saddleback roof with two sloping planes at the short ends.

ANKE

"Here you see Anke Kranendonk on the back of a moped. She lived near Bunschoten-Spakenburg. The woman driving helps them in the household, and is wearing a traditional Spakenburg costume."

Anke Kranendonk (1959) writes children's books.

THE CENTRE

The centre of Holland can be calculated in various ways. If you think of Holland as a square, the centre is in Soest. If you draw a circle around Holland, the centre is in Baarn.

This stone is on the Lindeboomsberg (Linden Tree Mountain) and was placed there in 1965 in response to a story told by an old farmer who claimed that before the draining of the IJsselmeer Polders (from 1926), there was as much land above this point as below it, and as much land to the west of it as to the east. In 2002, the original stone, which had cracked, was replaced with a new one.

DUTCH SPECIALTIES

A regional dish from the Achterhoek that has now reached the rest of Holland is the Achterhoek cinnamon rusk. Light dough is rolled out and cut into narrow strips. Sugar and cinnamon are sprinkled over them and they are then baked until crisp and traditionally served on Sunday.

Gazelle has been making bicycles in its bike factory since 1892. Today they produce more than 300,000 per year and are the market leaders in bicycle production. When the company reached its 100th anniversary, it was given the honor of "Royal" so that it is now Royal Gazelle.

NURSERY RHYME

On a big toadstool
Red with white dots
Sat the dwarf Spindlelegs
Rocking back and forth
Crack said then the toadstool
With the deepest sigh
Both those little legs
Up towards the sky

EXERCISE AREA

"In this region, there is a military exercise area. We almost forget that Holland has a real army."

The Dutch Armed Forces is made up of four units: the navy, the land forces, the air force, and the military police. There are currently around 45,000 service men and women.

At the moment, there is no conscription in Holland. If it were to be reintroduced, then around 2.8 million men in Holland could be called up.

The main duties of the armed forces are to defend the home territory and the allies, protecting and promoting international rule of law and stability, supporting the government in maintaining order, and providing emergency services and humanitarian aid both at home and abroad.

Chickens have been raised in the municipality of Barneveld since the 12th century. At the beginning of the 20th century, crossbreeding produced the famous Barnevelder chicken, a laying breed that can produce 180 to 200 brown eggs per year. The residents of Barneveld claim that a Barnevelder lays precisely 313 eggs per year—one on every day except Sunday. The weekly egg market in Barneveld sells 500 million eggs every year.

"The busiest amusement park in Holland is the Efteling, a unique park where you can see lots of fairy tales brought to life. Different people visit an amusement park—young, old, rich, poor, teens, families . . . In the zoo (which you will find in this book as well), you see parents with their children or grandparents with their grandchildren, but you won't see teens or young adults. Everyone goes to the amusement park. Something else that is typically Dutch are the terraced houses with a back garden. All the houses are the same size with the same shed, but people personalize things. Everybody chooses his or her own fence. Some people have a natural garden with winding paths, rabbits and birds, but you also have people who like order and completely measure their garden so that their plants are symmetrical and the paths are straight. At the bottom of the illustration I've drawn such a row of houses with all their similarities and differences."

SECOND HALF OF OCTOBER

THE AMUSEMENT PARK

THE EFTELING

The Efteling began as a playground. In 1952, the famous "Fairy Tale Forest" was opened. It was designed by Anton Pieck (1895-1978) and built by Peter Reijnders (1900-1974). "You must do something well or not do it at all," was Pieck's motto and a mark of his success is that sixty years later the Fairy Tale Wood is still the favorite part of the Efteling.

Since 1966, the Efteling has introduced a new attraction almost every year. Anton Pieck's successor, creative director Ton van de Ven (1944), is largely responsible. In addition to a magical Fairy Tale Forest, there is a constantly expanding park with spectacular and thrilling rides. The "World of Wonders" now has a hotel, a holiday park, a golf course, its own radio station, television studio, and a theatre.

"This is a maze for small children. When people talk about the Efteling, they never seem to pay any attention to the maze, so I thought I would put it right in the middle. You can trace the route from the beginning with your finger and if you do it right, you'll come to the exit."
The Adventure Maze designed by Harry Knoet (1942) was opened in 1995.

"They have several roller coasters in the Efteling. I admit they are difficult, but I still enjoy drawing them. If I take a ride on one, I come out looking green, so I've also included somebody like that, just like older people who really enjoy it

and younger people who find it really scary."
The Flying Dutchman is an attraction based on the legend of the same name (see p. 3): the public first walk through a haunted house and take their place in a roller coaster for a so-called *thrill ride*. The attraction was opened in 2007 and the design was by Karel Willemen (1967).

George and the Dragon is a double wooden roller coaster that replaced Pegasus in 2010. Pegasus had started to develop too many problems. Karel Willemen designed the attraction based on the legend of St. George who is said to have defeated a dragon (the symbol of heathenism).

When the Python opened in 1981, it was the longest roller coaster in Europe. It is 820 yards long, has two loop-the-loops and two corkscrews and reaches a top speed of 50 mph. Copies can be found in Italy, France and Venezuela.
In 2011, the attraction was given

a facelift and since then, a bright red snake races along the track.

"Here an elf is flapping around because she has escaped from the Dream Flight attraction."
Dream Flight is a so-called darkride. The spectators ride in gondolas over a 450-yard track through a world of elves and trolls designed by Ton van de Ven. Dream Flight opened in 1993.

"There is also a flying carpet in the Efteling. In reality, it is attached to a wire, but this was my chance to let things happen that never exist in reality."

In 1958, the Fakir, designed by Peter Reijnders, made his first flight over almost invisible wires. The Fakir flies back and forth between two towers. Where he plays the flute, tulips come into bloom.

"Here you see Snow White's seven dwarves taking a stroll."
In the Efteling, the seven dwarves have been grieving in front of Snow White's glass coffin since 1952.

The gnome village has been in the Fairy Tale Forest since its opening in 1952.

Dragon Easily Irritated becomes furious if somebody touches his treasure chest. There is no fairy tale about the dragon—he was thought up by Ton van de Ven—but he has become a terrifying favorite since his unveiling in 1979.

Long Neck has been in the Fairy Tale Forest since the very beginning and is one of the icons of the Efteling. He appears in the story of "The six servants" and was originally designed by Anton Pieck. The current version dates from 1979 and was designed by Ton van de Ven. In the winter, Long Neck wears earmuffs.

Gold-Ass—the donkey from the fairy tale "The Wishing-Table, the Gold-Ass, and the Cudgel in the Sack"—has been pooping golden Efteling coins since 1956. You have to insert a coin yourself.

This fountain has stood on the Anton Pieck Square since 1955 and portrays the goose girl from the Grimm fairy tale of the same name.

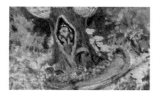

The Troll King from the fairy tale of the same name was designed back in 1974 by Ton van de Ven, but was not created until fourteen years later. The talking and moving troll makes the earth in front of his tree tremble.

Sleeping Beauty's castle could be seen at the opening in 1952, but nobody lived there at that time. A year later, Sleeping Beauty and the sleeping cooks were added. In 1981, the wicked stepmother was also placed in the castle.

The fairy tale "The Indian Water Lilies" was written by the Belgian Queen Fabiola. The fairy tale was designed by Anton Pieck for the fifteenth anniversary of the opening of the Efteling and was the last fairy tale he worked on before he retired.

Pardoes was designed in 1989 by Henny Knoet. This magician and jester is the symbol of the Efteling. He is not anchored to a specific attraction, but strolls around the park.

The garbage-eating Holle Bolle Gijs (Big Mouth) is one of the best-known figures in the Efteling. He shouts at the visitors, "Paper here," sucks in the trash and then makes a sound (he says, "Thank you" or burps or something similar). Since 1958, twelve different Gijses have appeared in the park.

Tom Thumb tries to steal the seven league boots from the giant. The pair appeared in the Fairy Tale Forest in 1998 based on a design by Ton van de Ven.

"The Chinese Nightingale" is the last fairy tale in the path through the Fairy Tale Forest. Hans Christian Andersen (1805-1875) wrote it. This version, based on a design by Ton van de Ven, has been here since 1999 and replaced the earlier version that had graced the fairy tale park since 1952.

Carnival Festival opened in 1984. The trip past dolls illustrating various cultures from the whole world was designed by film producer Joop Geesink (1913-1984). The red jester Jokie and his purple bird Jet can be found in every country.

The Piraña wild water ride, based on Inca, Maya, and Aztec cultures, was opened in 1983, from a design by Ton van de Ven. The boats were christened with water specially flown in from Peru.

Steam trains has run through the Efteling since 1968. People can get on and off at two stations. The three steam engines still running in the Efteling date from 1908 (Moortje), 1911 (Aagje) and 1992 (Trijntje).

The interactive Fairy Tale Tree has been telling fairy tales to the visitors to the Fairy Tale Forest since 2010. Karel Willemen (1967) designed it, based on drawings by Wil Raymakers. The 30-foot tall tree has 1,500 branches and twigs and 50,000 leaves. The Fairy Tale Tree also appeared earlier—from 2006 onwards—as the narrator in an animation series of the same name based on figures from the Fairy Tale Forest. The TV series can be seen in both Holland and Germany.

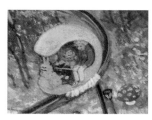

The witch has imprisoned Hansel, and Gretel must work for her. In 1977, this fairy tale from the park's earliest days was revamped by Ton van de Ven after consultation with Anton Pieck.

The People of Laaf were conceived by Ton van de Ven. Since 1990, you can wander through the village of the people of Laaf or view it from above during a trip on a monorail. At the introduction, the cars on the monorail had to be pedaled by their passengers, but now they move automatically.

The rocking ship The Half Moon swings out more than 25 yards and has a top speed of 33 miles per hour. The largest rocking ship in the world opened in 1982 and was designed by Ton van de Ven.

OTHER AMUSEMENTS PARKS

"I have drawn the song 'Ride, ride, ride in a little pram' with a pram that no longer exists and an old-fashioned girl with ribbons in her hair. In this way, the viewer immediately knows that something anachronistic and that helps them figure out the song.'

Ride, ride,
    ride in a little pram
If you don't want to ride
    I'll carry you
Ride, ride,
    ride in a little pram
And if you don't want to ride
    I'll carry you

CHARLES V

C CHARLES V (1500-1558)
THE NETHERLANDS AS
GOVERNMENTAL UNIT
At the age of fifteen, Charles V became the Lord of the Netherlands. A year later he was king of Spain and the Spanish colonies, and at the age of nineteen he also became emperor of Germany. At that time, the Hapsburg Netherlands were individual regions, each with their own laws and rules. Charles V conquered what is now Groningen and Gelderland and tried to turn the collective Netherlands into one state with one religion of Roman Catholicism. In the meantime, Charles V had become involved in all sorts of wars throughout his enormous empire. The costs were paid for in a large part by the prosperous Netherlands.
Not all the Dutch were happy with the united state—uprisings broke out against the high taxes and the nobility resisted attempts to restrict their power. They also rebelled against the one common religion believing that various (Christian) faiths could be tolerated. Despite all these protests, Charles V, who abdicated in 1555, is considered the founder of Holland as a governmental unit.

"Just when I finished the Efteling, I thought that all the other amusement parks in Holland would perhaps say, 'Hello. And what about us?' That is why I made an advertising sign for the other big amusement parks."
The observation tower "Princes Juliana Tower" opened in 1910, but during the Second World War the Germans ordered it to be renamed as "Julia Tower." What began with the erection of laughing mirrors as an extra attraction grew into a family amusement park with more than sixty attractions.

The Drievliet country estate has been around from the beginning of the 17th century. In 1952, a playground was opened which, as the years passed, was expanded with fairground attractions. In the 1990s, an experiment was made with thrill rides in order to attract a younger public.

Slagharen began in 1963 as a holiday park where people could rent a cottage together with a pony and cart. Very soon, a playground and a swimming pool were added and

more and bigger attractions were built for all ages. Today, Slagharen Attraction & Holiday Park attracts 1.5 million visitors per year.

Walibi began in 1971 as the educational amusement park Flevohof, but when the Flevohof went bankrupt, Walibi opened in 1994 as an attraction park. For a number of years, it was operated as the rollercoaster park Six Flags Holland, targeting teenagers. Today, the park has been extended further and is now known as Walibi Holland, suitable for everybody from the age of eight upwards.

Duinrell Estate was opened to the public in 1935. It offered a tea garden and a playground. The Tikibad—a tropical swimming pool with eleven water chutes—was opened in 1984. From then on, major attractions for both children and adults were added at a rapid rate. There is also a miniature golf course and an indoor playground.

Toverland Attraction park in Noord-Limburg was opened in 2001. It has two enormous halls: the Land of Toos for smaller children, and the Magic Forest for older children. In

addition, there is an outdoor park with attractions including a large roller coaster and a wild water ride.

The Sprookjeswonderland (Fairy Tale Wonderland) in Enkhuizen is a fairy tale world for families with young children. In addition to moving fairy tale figures, there is also a playground and attractions with a fairy tale theme.

In 1936, a recreation center consisting of a teahouse and playground was opened in Hellendoorn. A fairy tale garden and maze were added in 1956. Since the end of the 1970s, the adventure park has expanded rapidly, adding new, ever-larger attractions almost every year. Hellendoorn also organizes stunt shows and annual events. In Verkeerspark (Traffic Park) Assen,

children can drive cars themselves and learn how traffic works. This is the largest kiddie car park in Europe, and the children drive pedal cars, carts, and jeeps, as well as steer boats and make a trip in a train.

Every week from 2001 to 2012, a story appeared in the newspaper NRC *Handelsblad* about a fox terrier named Rintje that was written and drawn by Sieb Posthuma (1960). The stories were also published in various books.

"This is Marianna van Tuinen, a lesser-known artist but an exceptionally fine woman. I insisted that she appear here." The book entitled *The Rainbow Dolphin* was written by Marianna van Tuinen (1951) and published in 2012.

CARAVAN

"Holland also has something unusual in that people sometimes live in caravans. The strange thing is you never see them move house. I don't really know what the wheels are for, because they build around them. It could just be me." In Holland, around 30,000 people live in caravans or trailers. Since 1978, it is obligatory for these caravan dwellers to live in large centers or camps because law forbids traveling around. The majority of these people are descendants of Dutch peat diggers or laborers who travel the country in search of work.

NEIGHBORS

"The gardens of the terraced houses create a peculiar problem when a tree grows over the neighbor's garden. Some Dutch people don't like that, so what do they do? They saw off the branches hanging over their fence. I really hate it when somebody does that, so I thought, 'I'll get you.' The women are arguing with each other while the man is cutting off branches, but with all the tension he hasn't noticed that he's put the ladder down wrong. It could end up badly for him."

"It's November. Fortunately you have mist in November so I had a completely new range of colors, and that's good because otherwise I'll get bored. What do the Dutch eat? A French friend who is married to my Dutch sister-in-law, asked, 'Have you ever eaten that nasty green stuff?' I responded, 'But that's curly kale and it's really good!' That sort of food isn't sent abroad and so it mustn't be missing here.

However, the little people in this book are really tiny: I couldn't show a child eating a peanut butter sandwich because you wouldn't recognize it. Then I thought of the trucks that transported the food. If I could create a massive traffic jam with a whole lot of trucks crowded together, I could show all my Dutch food at once. In Holland you have roads everywhere and they even build them over each other so I had a great place for my traffic jam. But what about the reason for the traffic tie-up? I couldn't have a cow on the road because the road was in the sky and no cow would use it. However, a good accident wasn't a bad idea and that meant I could also have the ANWB helicopter fly in and all those sort of things."

THE MIST FIRST HALF OF NOVEMBER

HISTORY

C MAX HAVELAAR
(1860)
CHARGES AGAINST ABUSE IN INDONESIA

Eduard Douwes Dekker (1820-1887) worked in the Dutch East Indies from the age of 19 as civil servant and ultimately as assistant-resident. He couldn't bear the way the local population were exploited by the Dutch and Indonesian rulers. Because of this, he regularly fought with his superiors and returned to Europe when he was 38.

Using the pseudonym of Multatuli, he wrote the novel *Max Havelaar: Of De koffij-veilingen der Nederlandsche Handel-Maatschappij* (*Max Havelaar or The Coffee Auctions of the Dutch Trading Company*) where he was very critical of the administration in the Dutch East Indies. As soon as the first people read the manuscript, it became clear that the book would cause a stir. The government offered Douwes Dekker a very good job in the West Indies if he stopped the publication of the book. He refused.

In 1860, the book appeared for the price of four guilders, far beyond the reach of ordinary people. What's more, a number of names and places were also changed. Even so, *Max Havelaar* was a success throughout Europe.

In 1999, the famous Indonesian author Pramoedja Ananta Toer (1925-2006) called *Max Havelaar* "the book that put an end to colonialism."

"This is a poster for Fort Pampus in the Dutch Water Line. Forts were built throughout the country all the way to Utrecht. The idea was to flood the whole area if the enemy attacked."

In 1874, the decision was taken to lay a water line around Amsterdam that came to be called the Defense Line of Amsterdam. If Amsterdam were attacked, part of the city would be flooded to impede the enemy. Forts that would place the enemy under fire protected those places where the enemy could pass through.

The Pampus fort island is one of the 45 forts that were built for the Defense Line of Amsterdam. It was completed in 1895. Soldiers were only posted here during the First World War (1914-1918), but not a single shot was ever fired. Today, the island is open to the public and houses a museum about the Defense Line of Amsterdam.

"I solved Srebrenica with graffiti. It was so horrible that you can't draw it. I also think it shouldn't be included in the lessons for primary schools. That's a scandal. Wait until secondary school until you deal with something like that."

C SREBRENICA (1995)
THE DILEMMAS OF PEACEKEEPING

Since 1948, the Dutch have taken part in the so-called "peace missions" of the United Nations. For these operations, the Dutch Lower Chamber decides what the military's tasks shall be during the mission, and what it may or may not do.

In December 1993, a group of Dutch soldiers, known as "Dutchbat", were sent to Srebrenica in Bosnia. They had to protect a Moslem enclave against Serbian attacks. The Dutchbatters were only lightly armed because heavier arms could be seen as provocative and they were given instructions not to shoot at Serbians.

When, in the middle of 1995, there was the threat of a major Serbian attack, the Dutchbat made no less than four requests for air cover. None came, and the Serbians conquered the Moslem enclave without too much difficulty. They had the Dutch soldiers leave and killed all the Moslem men—more than 7,000—in the enclave.

The events raised many questions, and an official investigation was held in Holland. Several conclusions were that the soldiers were sent to Srebrenica with a bad mandate, insufficient preparation and inadequate equipment. This was severe criticism of the government and the military leadership. When the conclusions of the report were published in 2002, Prime Minister Kok submitted the resignation of his government.

FIGURES FROM CHILDREN'S LITERATURE

"Here's Harry Potter."
Harry Potter is the main character in the seven-part book series of the same name (1997-2007) by J.K. Rowling (1965).

"This is Mister Piggy by Gitte Spee, a friend from school."
Gitte Spee (1950) began her series of Mister Piggy books in 1988 with *Meneer Big gaat naar de maan* (*Mister Piggy Goes to the Moon*).

Cartoonist Jean Dulieu (1921-2006) drew Paulus de Boskabouter (Paulus the Woodgnome) for the first time in 1946 for the newspaper *Het Vrije Volk* (*The Free Peolple*). All in all, he drew 23 stories, each with a hundred episodes. Between 1955 and 1964 no fewer than 900 radio plays about Paulus the Woodgnome were broadcast. Two puppet series were shown on television in 1967 and 1974/75.

DUTCH SPECIALTIES

Coffee farmers from Mexico have said that they would prefer to receive an honest price for their coffee than development aid. That was the reason for Frans van de Hoff (1939), who was working as a missionary in Mexico, and Nico Roozen (1953), the director of development organization Solidaridad, to set up in 1988 the Max Havelaar Foundation to be a quality label for fair trade.

Every producer can apply for the Max Havelaar quality label for his product. After an assessment by an independent organization that investigates whether the raw materials of the product are produced and traded in compliance with the Fair trade standards, a decision is taken whether to grant the product the label. There are now more than 1,700 products with the label.

Boerenkoolstamppot—also called in Dutch *mous, moos, boeremoos,* or *boeremoes*—is curly kale and mashed potatoes mixed together with butter to make it creamy and a bit of salt and pepper. Traditionally, the mash is eaten with fried cubes of bacon and smoked sausage.

Curly kale is at its best if there has been a heavy ground frost while the kale is still on the land. This mash is also eaten in Northern Germany and Scandinavia.

The Dutch have eaten oil balls (formerly known as "oil cakes") for centuries to celebrate New Year. For the rest of the year, the treat—a fried ball of batter containing yeast—is only sold at fairs and festivals. The Dutch prefer the currant ball (oil balls with raisins or currants and sometimes apple) while the Flemish prefer a plain oil ball without any additions.

From the start of the 19th century, people in Gouda would use dough or cake leftovers to make "treacle waffles" or "syrup waffles" which are two thin wafers stuck together with treacle. These biscuits were also known as "poor cakes" because they were so cheap. Since 1870, treacle waffles have also been produced outside Gouda.

The Dutch "ordinary" or "gray" shrimp is a small shrimp that is caught in the North Sea. They are cooked immediately after they are hauled aboard the ship. As they cook, the grey shrimps get their characteristic pink color and curl up. The largest part of the catch is transported for peeling to Morocco where the wages are much lower.

The word *pindakaas* (peanut butter) was already used in Holland in 1901. It probably came from Suriname, where a thick peanut paste (*pindadokun*) was eaten on bread as early as the 18th century. The peanut butter people now know in Holland first appeared on the Dutch market in 1948 imported from the United States. It has become a favorite spread for bread.

The Dutch artist Wim T. Schippers (1942) caused something of a controversy with his artwork *Peanut Butter Floor* (1962), which featured a section of a floor spread with peanut butter. The artwork has been shown in various museums.

According to legend, St. Nicholas met three girls who were forced by their father to work as prostitutes because he could not pay their dowry. St. Nicholas threw them enough coins to provide them with a good dowry.

Today, when Sinterklaas passes by, his "Piets" throw around pepper nuts and sugar sweets or chocolate coins. In the past, they would throw pepper nuts and real coins. St. Nicholas is also the patron saint of marriage and family. Traditionally at Sinterklaas, boys would give marzipan to the girl they liked best. Unmarried ladies were teased with dolls made of *taaitaai* (a type of gingerbread) so that they at least had somebody to comfort them.

Chocolate was brought to Holland during the Eighty Years' War (1568-1648) by the Spanish occupiers. Coffee and chocolate houses opened where people could drink coffee or hot chocolate (*seculatie*).

It was not until the middle of the 19th century that chocolate was made into edible products, partly due to the invention of the Dutchman Casparus van Houten Sr. (1757-1858), who, in 1828, discovered how easily the fat could be separated from the cacao mass to create the cacao powder that is the base of all chocolate products. Van Houten is still a major Dutch chocolate manufacturer, just like Droste, Verkade, and Venz.

Sprinkles on bread (known as *hagel,* "hail") is typically Dutch. Small, long grains of chocolate (milk, pure, or mixed) are shaken over a slice of buttered bread and settle "like hail." Sprinkles with fruit-flavored sugar are also known as "fruit hail."

The chocolate maker Venz was the first company to market sprinkles in 1936, at the request of a five-year-old boy who asked for a sandwich topping made of chocolate.

Martien Breij (1884-1945) thought up the name "Chocomel" in 1932. After the Second World War, Nutricia, a dairy company with headquarters in Zoetermeer, became the owner of the name. Today, Chocomel (chocolate milk) is made in Belgium by Friesland-Campina.

The name Chocomel is now so well known that it is often used as a generic name for chocolate milk.

The ANWB was founded in 1883 as a bicycle association. Ten years later, legal aid assistance was added as a service. As time passed, the association expanded with car-drivers, horse-riders, pedestrians, water-sports enthusiasts, winter sports people, and campers.

Important sections of the association are now the Wegenwacht (Road Watch) that offer members helps when their cars break down, the Emergency Exchange for problems abroad, and international legal aid. The ANWB also provides traffic information on many Dutch radio stations. The ANWB has nearly four million members, making it the largest association in Holland.

In 1907, the Royal Dutch Petroleum Company merged with the English Shell Transport and Trading Company and formed the Royal/Shell Group. In 2005 the name was changed to Royal Dutch Shell.

Shell's headquarters are located in The Hague. The company handles all aspects of exploration, extraction, and processing of natural gas and oil.

In 2012, Shell topped the list of the world's largest companies, with a turnover of $484 billion and a payroll of 90,000 people throughout the world.

Frederick Henri Kay Henrion designed the familiar logo of KLM with the royal crown in 1961. Thirty years later, Chris Ludlow, who worked together with Henrion, tightened up the design a bit.

There are two official KLM blues. The light blue is Pantone 299 and the darker blue Pantone 541. These are the only two blues that may be used in the company's branding.

JAMMED

"When I was drawing the traffic jam I wondered how an ambulance get to it all? I went to a motorcycle agent to ask him how they did it.
'I've got an idea,' I said to him. He looked surprised: 'Oh?'
I explained, 'If the traffic is blocked up here because of an accident, then nobody will be driving further on. I think you'd close off the next exit and drive in the opposite direction to the traffic.' He looked at me and said, 'Yes, that's it.'
I had the feeling that my conclusion didn't really please him. I didn't even dare to turn round, so I thanked him and backed out of his way.
That's why I've drawn two red crosses above the road. Drivers may not drive any farther. Intentionally."

AQUEDUCT

The Ring Canal Aqueduct Haarlemmermeer carries the ring canal over the A4 highway. There are two Ring Canal Aqueducts, one for the high-speed railway and another for the expansion of the A4.

SAINT MARTIN AND SINTERKLAAS

"11 November is the day of lights. Here, mothers and fathers with children holding lanterns behind them are going to school. We see them there a little bit further along but those people will have to hurry because they're a bit late."
On 11 November, the Dutch celebrate St. Martin. Children go from door to door with lanterns to sing a song and ask for something tasty. The song goes as follows:

St. Martin, St. Martin
The cows all have tails
The girls are wearing dresses
And there comes St. Martin

The begging tradition is very old. In the Middle Ages, boys with torches would go from door to door on St. Martin. They beat on the doors with sticks and received a piece of fruit, some nuts, or some change.

"In November, Sinterklaas arrives."
Since 1952, the national entry of Sinterklaas has been shown on Dutch television. It is the moment that Sinterklaas and his Black Piets arrive in Holland from Spain on the steamboat.
The first twelve years he arrived in Amsterdam and once in Rotterdam, but since 1964 he has arrived at a different harbor each year.
Nowadays, the entry is on the first Saturday after St. Martin. In addition to the national entry, most cities and villages organize their own arrival, for which not only boat and horse are used, but also a strange collection of vehicles. Local entries never take place before the national entry.
The national entry marks the start of the Sinterklaas period and children are allowed to put out their shoes near the chimney in hope for sweets or presents.

DE CRUQUIUS

"This is De Cruquius, a steam mill. It stands on a dyke. The steam mill pumped the water up from below. They used to do this with windmills and today they use electric mills though the steam mills still work. An updated version is located not far from this steam mill."
The steam mill De Cruquius (1849) and two other mills pumped out the water from the Haarlemmermeer between 1849 and 1852. Until 1912, it was used to keep the polder dry, and then, until 1933, it was retained as a reserve mill.
De Cruquius is named after the hydraulic engineer Nicolaus Samuelus Cruquius (1678-1754), who, in his time, was concerned about the rise in the seawater and realized that the Haarlemmermeer would have to be drained because the water threatened Leiden and Haarlem.
Today, De Cruquius is a museum.

NURSERY RHYME

"In Haarlem, the children at school are taught a song, 'A Crocodile Lay Under the Bridge'."

Under the bridge of Spaarne,
A crocodile lay there.
Everyone who came along
Was bitten in his bum.
Ouch mister crocodile,
I'll get the police.
Then you'll have to pay for my bum.

HOUSE FOR SALE

"The Dutch build everywhere. Even if you have a maze of roads around you, you can still build your own house here. They just haven't managed to sell the plot yet."

CIRCUS

"You can also see the Renz Circus on the road. They always come to perform in Haarlem in the winter. I once came across them when I was driving home really late from Rotterdam. There was nobody else on the road and then there was suddenly a mile of Renz Circus. I overtook them very softly, in the hope of hearing the lions or something like that. However, you don't hear anything because the animals are all locked up. Traveling is stressful for them."
Renz Circus was founded in 1911. "Renz" means "Ras Echte Nederlandse Zwervers" (Completely Genuine Dutch Drifters). Today the circus visits some fifty cities each year and drives around 5,000 miles. It is one of the top three best and largest cicuses in Europe.

LEVELED

"I wanted to make a highway and a train track, but wondered how could they cross each other. They can't, because the train always travels at one level in Holland and it hardly ever climbs. The other traffic either goes over it or under it and there are few roads that cross the track. I think that's really unusual. In France, you've got whole sections where the train ascends, and you really feel it when you're in it."

RING CANAL

"This is the ring canal near Haarlem. The Dutch thought their country was too small

and concluded that if they pumped out the water, they would get a bit more country."
The ring canal is 37 miles long and was dug by hand between 1839 and 1945. The ring canal

carried away the water that had been pumped from the Haarlemmermeer by the mills.

"Limburg is totally different than the rest of Holland. It is the only region that is hilly and mountainous so it needed a special illustration. This is the interior so there is not a bit of sea around. Plus, it hangs, as it were, in Belgium. They also do something I think very special in that they extract black and white from the ground—coal and marl."

LIMBURG SECOND HALF OF NOVEMBER

THE ROMANS

"Limburg was attacked long ago by the Romans who built garrisons there. Things went well for a long time, but in the end, fighting broke out between the Batavians and the Romans. Here you see a Roman fortress and a piece of a prehistoric Batavia village."

C THE ROMAN LIMES (47-c. 400)
ON THE BORDER OF THE ROMAN WORLD

The Limes (Latin for "borders") of the Roman Empire ran across Holland known then as the Low Countries. Below the Rhine was Roman territory, and above the Rhine lived Teutons, Frisians, Saxons, and other Celtic tribes.
The Romans had lookout posts and small army camps along the Rhine, which were there to protect the Empire from attack. A camp was built near Nijmegen, then called Noviomagus, for 12,000 Roman soldiers.

Batavians also lived in the Roman territory. They lived in harmony until the Batavian Julius Civilis (25-?) led a revolt to avenge the death of his brother who had been executed by the Romans. Arnhem and Nijmegen were conquered with the help of the Teutons in AD 69, but a year later they themselves were defeated.
It was not until around AD 400 that the Romans withdrew from the Low Countries, finally driven out by the Teutons.

COAL, MARL AND FLINT

"There were flint mines back in prehistoric times. The men made a shaft in the ground until they reached a layer of soil with stones and then dug out the stones on the sides of the shaft. At the top they made a hoisting system with a beam. A friend lowered you into the shaft and hoisted you out with your stones. It was actually very dangerous, for if the friend suddenly decided that he was angry with you, you wouldn't be able to get out again."

"These are the marl pits of the past."
The Romans excavated marl in Limburg more than 2,000 years ago. Marl is a limestone that is very suitable as a building material since is strong, cheap, insulates well, and can be easily processed. Because the marl was excavated from between stone layers, a series of caves was formed that are today used for mushroom-growing efforts or housing bats. Tours are also given. Today, marl is only excavated in the Sibbe pit near Valkenburg-aan-de-Geul.

"This is an old coalmine. It is the last remaining mine shaft in Heerlen and houses a mine museum.
I thought this was a good place for providing a window into the history of child labor. It turned out that the mining industry in South Limburg only began after the Children's Law was introduced and children below twelve years of age were not allowed to work. The children you see working here are somewhat older, while the young ones are all still at home with mom, and she's doing the washing."
Coal was already being mined near Kerkrade in the 12th century and the first industrial coal mines opened around 1900. Coal was mined both by private companies and the government. By the beginning of the 1960s, coal mining became unprofitable, and all the mines closed between 1965 and 1974. The old mine shaft called Shaft II of the Oranje-Nassau Mine in Heerlen has been turned into the Dutch Mine Museum.

Flints are stones that are used to create sparks and fire. They were also used to make arrowheads, axes, and knives.

BONNEFANTEN MUSEUM

The Bonnefanten Museum in Maastricht owes its name to the convent that was located here for many years: "*Le couvent des bon enfants*" ("The convent of the good children"). In 1884, an archaeological museum was opened here. Today, the collection consists of both old and contemporary visual arts. Since 1995 it has been housed in a building on the River Meuse designed by the Italian architect Aldo Rossi (1931-1997).

FIGURE FROM CHILDREN'S LITERATURE

Alfie the Werewolf is the main character in the series of books of the same name by Paul van Loon (1955), the first of which appeared in 1996.

BE-NL-DE

"Vaals has the Three—Country Point, where three countries touch each other: Belgium, Holland, and Germany."

The Three-Country Point is on the highest spot in Holland (1,000 feet above sea level), on the top of the Vaalserberg (Vaals Mountain).

THE BUCKRIDERS

"The caves used to be the home of a whole gang of robbers known as the Buckriders. This is a wonderful, but also nasty story. The Buckriders were ordinary people with a respectable life who became robbers by night. They gathered in a cave and from there they attacked farms. They tortured people and eventually they were captured."

In the 18th century, a large gang made use of the superstitious fear of the mythological "buckriders": evil spirits who road on goats through the air. The most important motive for the crimes and robberies committed by the gang was simply poverty.

In the end, 600 people were sentenced in three periods, but because those arrested were tortured, a lot of innocent people may have confessed. The vast majority of them were given the death penalty.

DUTCH SPECIALTIES

Wine was made in Limburg for centuries but that stopped in the 19th century, because, according to the stories, Napoleon had the vineyards in Limburg destroyed. Today, thanks to the fertile marl ground, around 75,000 bottles of Limburg wine are produced each year.

Lottum, the "rose village of Holland," supplies around 20 million or 70% of all Dutch roses. The Rose Festival is held every other year and during the festival, flower arrangements are placed throughout the village. In addition, there is a Top Roses Garden and a rose bike route.

The "white gold'"(asparagus) has only been grown in Limburg since after the World War I. It proved such a success that its cultivation in the rest of Holland, which had been taking place since the middle ages, slowly declined. The asparagus season runs from 1 May to St. John's (24 June).

A *vlaai* is a flan-like pie made from soft bread-like dough, generally filled with fruit or rice. Originally the pie was eaten without whipped cream. The Limburg *vlaai* is baked in one go, with filling already added, and not combined later.

The state company DSM (Dutch State Mines) was founded in 1902 to mine coal in Limburg. Over the years, the company concentrated more and more on chemicals and petrochemicals. Since 1996, the Dutch State no longer has any shares in DSM. Today, the company concentrates on products for the food processing industry, the health care section, the automotive industry, the building industry, paint, and the production of bio-ethanol.

ARCHITECTURE

"The old farm buildings are different in Limburg than those in the rest of Holland—they were built slowly but surely in a square. It started with a normal house. When there was some more money, the following part was added and so on until all the sections together formed a square. Finally, the front door was removed from the original house and a gate was created. The entrance was then inside. This is a complete farm building."

The square farm building is also called a "square homestead." This building method has been used here since the 14th century.

Hoeve de Plei is a Tudor style farmhouse dating from 1740. This construction style, in which a skeleton of wooden beams is filled in with rods and loam or mortar, has been around for the last two thousand years. In Southern Limburg there are still Tudor style farmhouses that are three to four centuries old, thanks to the solid building style. The *plei*, which gave the farmhouse its name, can mean both "courtyard" and "a raised place

between two rivers." The farmhouse that now stands on the edge of the village of Mechelen used to be between the rivers Mechel and Geul. Hoeve de Plei is currently a hotel that has been renovated fully in traditional style.

Thorn in Limburg is also known as the "White Town." During the French occupation, a tax was introduced around 1800 that was set according to the size of a house's windows. Many poor people had their windows bricked up and then whitewashed the outside of their houses to hide the work that had been done to the brickwork (the "scars of poverty"). The white color has been retained for the houses in the town center of Thorn.

The Reus (Giant) of Schimmert is a 125-foot high water tower from 1927. Jos Wielders (1883-1949) designed it in the style of the Amsterdam School.

TRADITIONS AND FESTIVALS

find a small chapel or a cross with a Jesus figure."
The province of Limburg has no fewer than 2,200 crosses, 600 chapels, seventy holy grottos and a large number of individual crucifixion statues. These Catholic displays of piety were placed for various reasons such as gratitude, a memorial for a person or event, or in special locations, to mark where justice was meted out or a border.

"In November, people in Limburg start working on the floats for carnival."
In Limburg, they celebrate the so-called Rhineland carnival—it follows the traditions that have drifted over from Germany, in particular from Cologne. In 1823 Cologne, a *Maskenzug* was organized for the first time on the Monday after Shrove Tuesday. A procession of people wearing disguises, one of whom was chosen as "emperor", grew into the present carnival parades with people in costumes, decorated floats, and one Prince Carnival presiding over it all.

"In Limburg, people are more Catholic than Protestant. While I was making this illustration, the relic pilgrimage of St. Servaas was held in Maastricht. At first, I wanted to draw a procession with all the people, but they appeared to be so different in clothing that I had to conclude that this wasn't really my field."
St. Servatius (?-c. 384) was the first bishop of Maastricht and is the patron saint of the city. The relic pilgrimage—held once every seven years—goes back as far as 1391. It is a pilgrimage of several days in which the relics of St. Servatius are shown during a procession, and pilgrims are granted absolution (forgiveness for their sins).

"On many street corners and crossroads in Limburg you will

NURSERY RHYME

Say Red Riding Hood
Where are you going
All alone, all alone?
Say Red Riding Hood
Where are you going
All alone?

I'm taking my grannie
Some cookies
In the wood, in the wood
I'm taking my grannie
Some cookies
In the wood

MARY AND JOSEPH

"November is the time that Christmas starts getting closer. I've shown Mary and Joseph here—somewhat lost, but they are there."

WINTER SPORTS

Landgraaf boasts the largest covered winter sports village in the world, and the only existing indoor ski run with a competition license from the International Ski Federation (FIS).

KORENWOLF

The *korenwolf* is the Southern Limburg name for a colorful hamster that *woofs* (eats) corn. *Korenwoof* (corn woof) has become *Korenwolf* (corn wolf). The animal lives on leossial and loam soil, but, with the increasing amount of building and other agricultural cultivation, its existence is under threat. Attempts are now being made to help the population grow.

CHRISTMAS DECEMBER

TRADITIONS AND FESTIVALS

On December 6, the day after *pakjesavond* (the evening of Sinterklaas when presents are exchanged), Sinterklaas and his Piets return to Spain. This is not celebrated as extensively as his arrival in Holland, but locally the company is given a farewell.

"When Sinterklaas leaves, Father Christmas arrives."
Santa Claus, the American Father Christmas, actually comes from Holland. The Dutch colonists took the Sinterklaas festival to America in the 18th century where it developed into a festival with presents around Christmas with Santa Claus as the generous giver. A series of Coca-Cola advertisements in 1930 gave Father Christmas his current appearance.
This Father Christmas in turn came over from America to Europe, where he got more and more popular as the years went by. Since 2006, Father Christmas officially arrives in Holland the weekend after 5 December.

"At Christmas, the square in Gouda where the scales are located is lit with candles. That's why I painted a shop window with the Gouda Scales in it and a lot of candles."
The Gouda Scales were designed by architect and artist Pieter Post (1608-1669) and opened in 1668. At first, all sorts of goods were weighed on the scales, but, as time passed, they gradually specialized in weighing cheese. That's why the building is also known as the "Cheese Scales" and currently houses the Cheese and Crafts Museum.
Candles have been made in Gouda since 1853. Since 1956, "candle evening" has been held in the city on the second Tuesday in December. The lights in the streets and shops are turned off and the candles on the Christmas tree on the Market are lit. All the windows of the buildings in the area are aglow with the light from thousands of candles.

COMPOSERS

"People go to concerts in the winter. This is a great opportunity to mention a few Dutch composers I mustn't omit: Sweelinck, Willem de Fesch, Andriessen, and my favorite Simeon ten Holt."

Jan Pieterszoon Sweelinck (1562-1621) is considered the most important Dutch composer of Early Music during the transition from Renaissance to Baroque music. He was famous throughout the world during his lifetime and composed more than 250 pieces for ensemble and voice and more than seventy keyboard compositions.
Violinist **Willem de Fesch** (1687-1761) composed Baroque music. He wrote a large number of songs and composed a mass and two oratorios in addition to many sonatas for violin and flute and a number of concertos for violin and orchestra.
The Andriessen family has produced gifted composers for many generations. The best known is **Louis Andriessen** who is seen as the most influential composer of his generation. He rebels against existing traditions and blurs the boundaries between different genres. He received the prestigious Grawemeyer Award for Music Composition for his opera *La Commedia* (2004-2008).

During his life, **Simeon ten Holt** (1923-2012) grew to become one of the most famous minimalist composers. His best known work is *Canto Ostinato* (1976) for various combinations in which many decisions are left to the musicians themselves. Performances of Ten Holt's compositions are total experiences—a single piece can last hours. For example, in a performance of *Lemniscaat* (1983) both the pianists and the audience took turns, and the piece ultimately lasted a whole day.

DUTCH SPECIALTIES

"I once heard the man who makes the Febo croquette talking lyrically about it on the radio. 'Febo, the tastiest,' that's what they call the croquette. I put a roll next to it, for a croquette with a roll is also very Dutch."

A croquette is meat ragout in a breadcrumb coating that is deep-fried. The oldest recipe dates from 1691 and from a chef of the French Sun King. In Holland, the chef of King Willem I wrote down the recipe for the first time in 1830. Until the Second World War, it was an upper class dish, but later it became a favorite snack that can be eaten by hand or on a soft white roll with mustard. Baker and confectioner Febo came up with the idea of offering their much-loved croquettes in a vending machine.

"I find the Chinese culturally interesting. They add a Chinese touch to an ordinary Dutch house and it turns into a restaurant. The most important section is the take-away.
The Chinese signs on the door are real. There is a Chinese restau-

rant in Haarlem on the Zeilweg, and I copied the characters from there because a Chinese child must also be able to read this book."

After a major harbor strike in 1911, Dutch ship owners started employing more and more Chinese personnel who were willing to work for a low wage—so the first Chinese restaurants began in port cities (in 1920 in Rotterdam and in 1924 in Amsterdam). After the Second World War, many people who had lived in Indonesia returned to Holland and then lots of Chinese restaurants became "Chin.Ind.Rest."—Chinese Indonesian Restaurant.

Slowly but surely, The Chinese restaurants grew in popularity because you can eat a lot for a little money. At their high point of popularity in 2001, there were 2,400 Chinese restaurants in Holland. Now the number is declining rapidly, as restaurants from countries all over the world appear.

In 1887, Albert Heijn took over his father's grocery shop in Oostzaan.

In 1895, he started roasting coffee. During the next fifteen years, he opened more than ten branches, and in 1910 he started selling products with his own brand. A year later, Albert Heijn began producing cake and confectionery in his own kitchen. Thirty years after taking over his father's small business, the annual turnover of Albert Heijn's company had reached four million guilders. On its fortieth anniversary, the company—now in the hands of the sons of Heijn and son-in-law Hille—earned the name "Purveyor to the Royal Family." The company had, by then, begun to bottle its own wine and had its own chocolate factory.

In 1952, the first self-service shop opened and by 1959, the one hundredth was established. Albert Heijn continues to grow. Today there are AH To Go shops that are mini-supermarkets in places like train stations and hospitals. There is an online store with a delivery service and there are Pick Up Points—drive-thru locations where articles can be collected without leaving the car.

In 1926, the Hollandsche Eenheidsprijzen Maatschappij Amsterdam (HEMA—Dutch Unit Price Company Amsterdam): a department store where everything was on sale for 25 or 50

cents was established. Later, articles costing 10 and 75 cents and one guilder went on sale. The staff, mainly unmarried women, worked 75 hours each week. The wealthy turned up their noses at the shop and spoke about "Hier Eet Men Afval" ("here one eats garbage"). After World War II, the unit prices were discontinued but the HEMA was still seen as a cheap department store. It was also the first franchise organization in Holland. There are now 600 HEMA stores in the Benelux, Germany, and France. In 1936, one of branch managers

found he had bought too many smoked sausages. He heated them up and sold them as a snack. It was such a success that the HEMA sausage is now a permanent fixture in Dutch life.

In 1887, friends and brothers-in-law Willem Vroom (1850-1925) and Anton Dreesmann (1854-1934) opened a business in "manufactured and related articles." They sold articles for a low price for cash payment at a time

when much was sold on credit at higher prices. Because they were able to pay quickly, they could purchase very economically. The number of branches grew along with the range of products.

In 1912, Holland's first modern department store, V&D (Vroom & Dreesmann), opened in the Kalverstraat in Amsterdam. Today V&D has more than sixty branches and is the largest department store chain in Holland.

"Delft Blue is also typically Dutch but how could I show it? It's all so small. That's why I made a shop where they sell Delft Blue."

Delft Blue china has been made since the end of the 16th century, initially as an alternative for the much more expensive Chinese porcelain. Between 1650 and 1750, there were no fewer than one hundred ceramics factories in Delft producing Delft Blue. Around 1800, an even cheaper alternative arrived from England and the trade was finished. Now there is only one factory in Delft that produces Delft Blue ceramics.

FAMOUS DUTCH

Frans Hals (c. 1583-1666) was a painter in Haarlem who, along with Rembrandt, Jan Steen, and Johannes Vermeer, is considered an Old Dutch Master. Hals was known particularly for portraits of contemporaries and so-called "shooting club pieces" that were group portraits of riflemen's guilds. Riflemen were volunteers who joined together to keep the peace and to protect their village or town from attack from the outside.

The father of Johannes Enschedé (1708-1780), Izaak Enschedé (1681-1761), founded a printing shop in Haarlem in 1703, which concentrated mainly on

printing special projects such as books in Hebrew, Braille, or music notation. Johannes followed in his father's footsteps and, from 1743, the publisher became known as "Joh. Enschedé and sons." From 1769, the publisher printed shares and other bonds, and, from 1810, banknotes. Since 1866, the company has been printing postage stamps for several countries. They also printed the Dutch euro notes until 2011 but then the contract was placed into the hands of German and English printers.

NURSERY RHYME

Bye bye Sinterklaas bye bye
Bye bye Black Piet
Bye bye Sinterklaas bye bye
Listen to our goodbye song

CHRISTMAS CAROLS

FIGURES FROM CHILDREN'S LITERATURE

"A flight attendant is walking here who will be taking the bus or train to Schiphol. By chance, she finds Raf, a giraffe from a book by Anke de Vries."
Raf is the main character in the book of the same name written by Anke de Vries (1936) and illustrated by Charlotte Dematons (1957). It appeared in 2008.

"Kruimeltje (Little Crumb) is sitting by the church, completely covered in snow. Fortunately, he's saved."
Kruimeltje is the main character in the children's classic book of the same name by Chris van Abkoude (1880-1960), which appeared in 1923 and was successfully filmed in 1999 by Maria Peters (1958).

OUCH!

"The Dutch just cycle on through the snow, but things can sometimes go wrong."

WITCHES

"This is the Waag (Scales) of Oudewater where they weighed witches. A witch is only a witch if she doesn't weigh anything. The women who had themselves weighed in Oudewater all apparently had weight and so they were each given a certificate clearing them of witchcraft. In olden times, many women accused of witchcraft came to Oudewater to obtain such a certificate to avoid being burned. This is a tribute to those women."
The scales in Oudewater were built in 1482 to weigh goods. But in 1545 emperor Charles V gave official permission to weigh witches on it. This was the only place in Europe where this could take place. Women came from far and wide to have themselves weighed in Oudewater right into the 18th century. None was ever condemned as a witch. The Witch Scales is now a museum. The old scales are still there and visitors can have themselves weighed in order to receive a certificate that they are not witches.

"Every year in Haarlem at midnight on Christmas Eve, people come together on the Nieuwe Kerk Square to sing Christmas carols. Everybody can join in and that makes it very special."

"Something you see a lot at Christmas time is the Salvation Army Band. You hear music coming from somewhere, but you can't see anybody. Then you suddenly see them, standing in the dark."
The first Salvation Army meeting in Holland took place in 1887, under the leadership of Gerrit Govaars (1866-1954), with the aim of spreading the gospel and helping people in need. Soon after, depart- ments were started in the Dutch East Indies (1894), Suriname (1926) and Curaçao (1927). During the Second World War, when the Germans prohibited the Salvation Army, the organization officially became a "faith community," so that it could continue its activities under the Law on Church Communities. The Army today has 300 groups in Holland and more than 4,500 employees.

ARCHITECTURE

"In Holland there is a new trend where many churches are no longer used for religious services but instead have been adapted for housing."
The neo-gothic Heilig-Hart (Holy Heart) Church in Haarlem was built in 1902 as a Roman Catholic church, under the supervision of architect Peter Bekkers (1859-1918). In 1996, it was turned into apartments.

"Holland has many almshouses. Here I have shown an almshouse as it was in its early days with the women who lived there."
A Dutch almshouse consists of small houses around a central courtyard. Since the 13th century, the church or the philanthropic citizens paid for the building of almshouses. The houses were intended for poverty-stricken elderly married couples or women (men went to the old men's house) and for women who wanted to live a religious life without taking the vows of a nun (beguines). It cost nothing to live in an almshouse, but one was expected to live a devout and pious life.
In the second half of the 19th century and the first half of the 20th century, almshouses were still built for poor working class families. In Haarlem, twenty of the original forty almshouses still exist. It is ironic that the Haarlem Beguine Almshouse from 1262 is now used as a brothel.

STREET NEWS

"Here somebody is selling the Straatjournaal."
The Big Issue has been published in London since 1991, and Holland has its own version of the newspaper for the homeless sold by people without a fixed home or address. Utrecht was the first Dutch city with a newspaper, *Straatnieuws* (*Street News*) produced by the homeless. Other cities and regions quickly followed. The *Straatjournaal* (*Street Journal*) is the homeless newspaper for the regions of Haarlemmermeer, Kennemerland, West-Friesland, the Kop van Noord-Holland, and Texel.

"I really had problems with the Flevopolder. What could I show there? It's all new. Suddenly it came to me—I'd celebrate New Year's Eve in Almere! Everybody celebrates the New Year in his or her own way. There is a married couple that doesn't want anything to do with the neighbors and stays inside while everybody else celebrates together outside. That couple is celebrating it together, dressed very smartly. They also have one of those gardens with nothing in them except a fence to place your bike against. That sort of garden really does exist. You won't be able to find Black Piet in this picture. He's in the bathroom in the second house."

31 DECEMBER - 1 JANUARI

NEW YEAR'S EVE IN ALMERE

The Flevopolder, previously known as Flevoland, is actually an island because it is completely surrounded by water. The area was drained between 1955 and 1968 to provide a place for the growing population of Amsterdam. Almere has nearly 200,000 inhabitants, making it the largest city of the Flevopolder, and lies between two and five yards below sea level. "Almere" is the name used in the early Middle Ages for the Zuiderzee, the inland sea that used to be here.

HISTORY

"There's a poster hanging here about the North East Polder, with Schokland and Urk."

Schokland was an island in the Zuiderzee—one of the poorest municipalities in Holland. That's probably where the name came from. *Schokken* were packs of reed or dried cow dung, which were used by the poor for heating.

From the Middle Ages, the island grew smaller and smaller through storms and threatening water. That's why King Willem III decided in 1859 that it had to be evacuated. The whole population of 650 people had to find somewhere else to live. Only a few people remained on the island including a lighthouse keeper and some harbormasters.

The island became a popular destination for day tourists. In 1942, the North East Polder was drained and Schokland was no longer surrounded by water. Since 1995, this no-longer-an-island is on the World Heritage List of UNESCO.

Urk also began as an island and has been part of the North East Polder since it was drained in 1942. Even though Urk is no longer on the open sea, it still has by far the largest fishing fleet in Holland and is one of the most important fishery centers in Western Europe.

"Near Lelystad, the Batavia has been rebuilt on the Batavia Wharf."

The Batavia was a VOC ship that was to make its first trip to Batavia on Java in 1628. The ship never arrived— a thousand nautical miles from its destination; it ran aground on a reef near the Australian coast. A large part of the crew was able to find safety on an island. The commander of the ship, François Pelsaert (1595-1630), set off in a sloop with a number of officers to sail to Java for help. During his absence, deputy merchant Jeronimus Cornelisz (1598-1629) tried to found his own kingdom on the island, with himself at its head. He and his henchmen murdered more than a hundred men. When Pelsaert returned from Batavia to fetch his men, he saw what had happened. He had the offenders tried and they received the death penalty, whip lashes, or were keel hauled. Of the 341-man crew, only 68 actually reached Batavia.

A start was made on building a reconstruction of the Batavia in 1985, thanks to initiative by the master shipbuilder Willem Vos (1940). In 1995, Queen Beatrix christened the completed ship that can be visited daily on the Batavia Wharf in Lelystad.

ARCHITECTURE

"Almere is different than all other cities in Holland, because everything is new. Plots of land were sold where people could build houses they had designed themselves. You won't see that anywhere else. Two houses under one half ball. That's really Almere."

NURSERY RHYME

Saw, saw, wiedewiedewagen
Jan came home to ask for a
    sandwich
Father wasn't home
Mother wasn't home
Peep said the mouse in the
    front of the house

CLOSED

"Public post boxes and trash bins are closed up during New Year, to prevent firecrackers from being put in them."

SAFETY

Of course, during the firework night, the fire department is always ready. Reflecting white and blue diagonal stripes marks the red fire engines.

FIGURES FROM CHILDREN'S LITERATURE

"The Batavia could be nicely combined with De scheepsjongens van Bontekoe [The Ship-Boys of Bontekoe], which is also about the VOC."

Willem IJsbrantsz. Bontekoe (1587-1657) was a skipper for the VOC. His ship, carrying 350 barrels of gunpowder, caught fire in 1619 in the Sunda Strait and exploded. Bontekoe and part of his crew were able to reach Sumatra in a sloop, but there they were chased away by the local population. They chose to sail on the open sea, making a sail from their shirts and were rescued by a passing fleet.

Johan Fabricius (1899-1981) used this fact as the basis for his boys' book *The Ship-Boys of Bontekoe* dating from 1924 where it emerges that one of the ship's boys is responsible for the fire. The story gets a sequel with an adventure by the boys on Sumatra and their sea trip home. The book was filmed in 2007 by Steven de Jong (1962).

TRADITIONS AND FESTIVALS

The tradition of setting off fireworks on New Year's Eve in Holland goes back to the middle ages. Symbolically, the old year was chased away and the new year welcomed. That takes place in other Northern and Eastern European countries, but in Holland, they take it to a new level, setting off the most fireworks per member of the population. More than seventy million euro goes up in smoke.

In May 2000, a fire broke out in the firework depot in Enschede and 177 tons of fireworks exploded. Two hundred houses were completely destroyed and 2,000 buildings seriously damaged. There were 23 deaths and around 950 people were injured.

More and more frequently, discussion flares up about restricting the firework tradition or only allowing professional firework shows.

"Large bonfires, such as in Amsterdam—North, are also lit on New Year's Eve."

The large New Year fires go back to the period of the Teutons, some two thousand years ago. They had the twelve-day Yule Festival where they celebrated the passing of the period of darkness and welcomed the lengthening of days. One of these twelve days coincided with our January 1, when they lit large fires and sacrificed animals.

Many old Christmas trees end up on the fires at New Year but, every year, a number of cars are also set on fire.

"On New Year's Eve, they shoot carbide in the country. It causes an enormous bang. They really like it."

Carbide shooting takes place mainly in the north and east of Holland. Moistening the carbide causes the release of acetylene, an extremely flammable gas that is then ignited.

In the south of the country, carbide shooting traditionally takes place when a young couple gets engaged. The explosions are really deafening.

"From the festivities of December, we move on to the cold barrenness of January."

NEW YEAR ON
THE COAST

I JANUARY

TRADITIONS AND FESTIVALS

"On 1 January, some of the Dutch go crazy and they run —whether there's snow, wind or rain—into the sea. I have a friend who does it every year and on one stormy New Year's Eve, I asked her, 'There's a storm outside. You won't be going, will you?' 'What do you think! Of course I will!' came her answer."

The first New Year's Dip in Holland took place in 1960 in Zandvoort, followed by Scheveningen in 1965. The first dip in Scheveningen attracted seven people. Today, more than 10,000 people run into the sea at Scheveningen on 1 January, regardless of the weather. In 2007, however, the New Year's Dip in Scheveningen was canceled by order of the police, fire brigade, and emergency services because of the terrible weather conditions. A New Year's Dip is organized at about ninety places in Holland.

On Epiphany Evening, children go from door to door in groups of three with crowns on their heads. They carry lanterns and sing a song in exchange for sweets.

On Epiphany Day (Twelfth Night), 6 January, a special king's tart is baked—a sort of butter cake with almonds—in which a brown bean is hidden. The person who gets the slice with the bean is king of the house and his word is law.

"Somebody pointed out, 'Hey, you've forgotten the theater.' Here you see Gijsbrecht van Aemstel.*'*

Poet and playwright Joost van den Vondel (1587-1679) wrote the play *Gijsbrecht van Aemstel* for the opening of the Amsterdam City Theater in January 1638. It became a tradition to perform the piece annually on New Year's Day in the City Theater, and, with just a few exceptions, the tradition has continued for hundreds of years.

The complete title of the play is *Gysbregt van Aemstel, d'ondergang van zijn stad en zijn ballingschap. Treurspel. (Gysbregt van Aemstel, the Decline of his City and his Exile. Tragedy.)* The story is based on the historic figure Gijsbrecht IV, Lord of Amstel (c. 1230-1303), who—because he had participated in the murder of the very popular Floris V in 1296 (see p. 28)—was driven out of Amsterdam in 1303 by angry Dutch farmers.

"Beachcombing today by bike, and beachcombing in the past."

Salvaging wrecks, or *jutten* (beachcombing), is as old as shipping. People go to the beach in search of goods that have been washed ashore. Things may have been swept overboard or may have come into the water after a wreck. The beachcombers use these goods or sell them.

In the past, people would use a horse and cart for the job and anything found was tossed in. Today, the beachcombers load their finds into four-wheelers. You can also bike on the hard sand along the ebb line.

Beachcombing is actually forbidden—anything found on the beach should be given to the police or to a wreck master (a regulator), but that only makes the challenge all the more interesting for the beachcombers.

NURSERY RHYME

Say, do you know the mussel man
The mussel man, the mussel man
Say, do you know the mussel man
Who lives in Scheveningen?

Yes, I know the mussel man
The mussel man, the mussel man
Yes, I know the mussel man
Who lives in Scheveningen

We all know the mussel man
The mussel man, the mussel man
We all know the mussel man
Who lives in Scheveningen

The children stand in a circle. Two children stand opposite each other in the middle of the circle. During the first verse, one child swings one leg forward and then the other backward; in the second verse, the child opposite him jumps in the same way; during the third verse they take each other's hand and dance around in the circle while the other children clap.
When the song is over, the two children go and stand opposite two other children in the circle. This is repeated until all the children have danced.

This song has blown over from London, where children sing this song to the same melody:

Do you know the Muffin Man
The Muffin Man, the Muffin Man
Do you know the Muffin Man
Who lives on Drury Lane?

Three Kings, Three Kings
Give me a new hat
My old one is worn out
My mother mustn't know
My father has already
Counted the money on the counter

FINE ARTS

bankrupt, Mesdag bought back the panorama. It is still in the hands of his family.

"This panel is an advertisement for Panorama Mesdag *in The Hague."*
The *Panorama Mesdag* is the largest painting in Holland and is 15 yards high and 130 yards wide. It is painted in a round room so the viewer finds himself in the middle of the painting. Hendrik Willem Mesdag (1831-1915) painted this view over the North Sea, beach, dunes, The Hague and Scheveningen in 1881. It is one of the oldest panoramas in the world.
When the original client went

"This ship can be seen in the Teylers Museum in Haarlem. It is superbly painted."
Detail from *Storm at Sea* (1820-1825) by Johannes Christiaan Schotel (1787-1838)

ARCHITECTURE

"This lighthouse, and the houses in front of it, are in Scheveningen."
The 160-foot high wrought iron lighthouse of Scheveningen dates from 1875 and was designed by Quirinus Harder (1801-1880). The lamp has been powered by electricity since the 1960s and gives two light flashes per ten seconds that can be seen 32 miles away.

The Andreaskerk (Andrew's Church) on the Katwijk boulevard is also known as the Oude Kerk (Old Church) or White Church. It dates from c. 1640, but the point on the dome was erected in 1837 after the original spire was damaged beyond repair by a storm in

1836. The church is named after St. Andrew, the patron saint of fishermen.

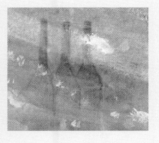

"These houses were stolen a little from Wijk aan Zee."

Since as far back as the 14th century, the Dutch have extracted shell lime (mortar) from shells. The limekiln of Katwijk aan Zee dates from 1934 and stopped burning lime in 1971.

"I wanted to include both the Kurhaus and the Pier of Scheveningen in the book. In my first attempt, I made the whole illustration from a different point of view, so that you could see them in the distance, but the rest had to be drawn so small that there was virtually nothing left to see. Now I have solved that by dedicating a panel to them. The Kurhaus is far too beautiful to be excluded and there's only one pier like this one in Scheveningen."
The Kurhaus opened in 1885 and was based on a design by the German architects Johann Friedrich Henkenhaf (1848-1908) and Friedrich Ebert (1850-1914).

It was built on the site of an old wooden bathhouse. The following year, the building burnt to the ground. After it was rebuilt in 1886, two international peace conferences were held there (in 1894 and 1899) and many VIPs have stayed there.
Celebrities such as Maria Callas, Duke Ellington, and Edith Piaf performed in the Kurhaus auditorium. The first concert given by the Rolling Stones in Holland was also held here but the performance had to be abandoned after just four songs because the audience had become hysterical.
Since 1979, the Kurhaus has belonged to the Steinberger Hotel Group.

The Pier of Scheveningen was opened in 1961. The promenade pier with three "islands" was designed by architects Huib Maaskant (1907-1977), Dick Apon (1926-2002) and Dirk Jan Dijk (?-1975). One of the islands has an observation tower. In 1964, a fourth island was attached to the pier, without the necessary building permit.
The catering company Van der Valk purchased the pier, which by then was very dilapidated, for one guilder and built restaurants, hotels, a casino, and party rooms on it. The future of the pier has become uncertain since a fire in September 2011. There is much overdue maintenance and its creditors have requested the holdings bankruptcy.

TRADITIONAL COSTUMES

"These women in traditional Scheveningen costumes are standing on the dyke, on the lookout for their fishing husbands."

"A woman from Scheveningen is walking here in traditional costume. The characteristic hat is made from a reed-like material. You don't see them very often today."

TO THE RESCUE

The national rescue team (The Royal Dutch Association for the Rescue of People from Drowning) consists of more than 180 independent associations. Their boats and cars can be recognized by the bright orange color and blue and white diagonal stripes. Holland water-land has had an official Company for Rescuing People from Drowning since 1767.

In 1893, the Amsterdam doctor C.B. Tilanus Jr. founded the Vereniging Eerste Hulp Bij Ongelukken (EHBO—Association First Aid For Accidents), which, in common with the English model, trains laypeople to give first aid. His colleagues in the medical profession were initially not pleased with this. They urged that nursing help had to be given by professionals.

In 1909, an initiative by Prince Hendrik resulted in the founding of The Orange Cross, a foundation for the promotion of EHBO (FIRST AID). The Orange Cross Book, which was first published in 1912, is still the basis for FIRST AID courses though it now has much more detail. Since 1951, participants who successfully complete this course are given a FIRST AID diploma.

DUTCH SPECIALTIES

In 1997, Unox—the company that is known for its smoked sausages and soups—served free thick pea soup to the participants and volunteers of the Eleven Cities Tour, together with an orange cap with the Unox logo. It was an enormous success. The Eleven Cities Tour is only held occasionally, and the Unox cap now mainly enjoys its fame because it is given free to all participants at the New Year's Dip.

Three former students of the Technical University in Delft thought up an asymmetrical umbrella. Thanks to its special shape, the umbrella always turns into the wind and can withstand quite a bit. The storm umbrella was introduced in 2006 under the name senz[0] and has won countless prizes, including the Gold International Design Excellence Award in 2008.

"When you come out of the seawater half-dead, you can go to this café for a free bowl of thick pea soup."

Thick pea soup—or *snert*—is a Dutch winter soup made from split peas. Other ingredients include pork, celery, leek, pepper, and salt. Many people also add potato and carrot to make the soup even thicker.

The soup is traditionally served with smoked sausage and rye bread with bacon. The oldest Dutch thick pea soup recipe dates from 1514.

EVERYTHING WHERE IT BELONGS

"Here, trash is no longer collected from the houses, but people sort them into bins themselves. There is one for general waste, one for paper, and one for glass."

According to the "National waste control plan," everybody in Holland has to separate the following types of waste: vegetable, fruit and garden waste; paper and cardboard; glass; textile, plastic packaging waste; electronic equipment; small chemical waste; and components from coarse household waste (such as coarse garden waste and household building and demolition waste, including preserved wood). The last three categories have to be offered separately. There are special waste bins for the first five.

"There are well placed trash bins everywhere on the beach."

FIGURE FROM CHILDREN'S LITERATURE

"This is Quibus by Ingrid and Dieter Schubert who are dear friends of ours."

Quibus plays the main role in the wordless picture book entitled *The Umbrella* from 2010 by the artist couple Ingrid (1953) and Dieter (1947) Schubert.

SURINAME

"To redress the balance with all that dreariness we see advertising for Suriname. It's nice and warm there and it is a topic of history."

See (p. 23) for the topic about Suriname and the Dutch Antilles.

DOG-WALKING SERVICE

"A dog-walking service is something else you have in Holland. I always thought that was decadent until I saw this man at his work. Now I say to everybody, 'Have you got a dog? Treat him once a week to a walk along the sea, because that's great!' The man throws a ball and all those dogs—big and small, fat and thin, hairy and smooth—rush off after it. There are very big dogs and very small dogs, but no dogfights. There are also dogs that seem to think, 'I don't feel like it.' They sit and stay next to the man. If you ask me, it's a treat for the animals."

VACANCIES

"The statement 'Zimmer Frei' really amuses me because it only says that there are vacant rooms in German and not in Dutch."

Most foreign tourists in Holland come from Germany. The annual number of German tourists is now almost three million, and the majority comes here for a stay on the Dutch coast.

"Holland is always fighting with the water. That is why, here in the middle of the book in the month of January, when everything is a little grey and dreary, I have shown the Flood of 1953. That was a terrible drama. After all these years, it is still painful for those who experienced it.
I thought it important to make a somewhat quieter illustration at this point in the book, because there has been so much going on until now. When I had finished this illustration, somebody asked, "Are you going to paint some boats?" No, for everything was completely quiet on the day after the flood. Everything had gone. It was dreary, gray, and miserable.
The dykes everywhere make Zeeland special. The roads are higher than the land. When the fields are ploughed, they take on a sort of fatty, gray-brown clay color. When the sun isn't shining, it is terribly gloomy. However, once the sun shines, everything becomes cheerful, even in the winter.
The town illustrated here is Veere."

ZEELAND AND THE FLOOD OF 1953

SECOND HALF OF JANUARY

NURSERY RHYME

"'Fetch two pails of water' seemed suitable for this situation."

Fetch two pails of water
Pump up two pails full
Girls on their wooden clogs
Girls on a wooden leg
Ride through my little street
From your race, race, race
The king rides through the place
From your fate, fate, fate
The king rides through the gate
From your lurch, lurch, lurch
The king rides through the church.
From your one, two, three!

C THE FLOOD (1 february 1953)

THE THREAT OF THE WATER

In the night of 31 January on 1 February 1953, a combination of spring tide and a northwesterly storm caused a flood of unprecedented height known as the St. Ignatius Flood. The dykes in the estuary could not resist the pressure of the water. People had known for thirty years that the dykes were too weak, but because of the depression and the Second World War, improvements took place slowly. The area that was most heavily hit by the flood was the next in line for improvement.

The enormous flooding that followed submerged the main part of Schou-wen-Duiveland and Goeree-Overflakkee, together with areas of North and South Beveland, West Brabant, and South Holland. There were around 1,800 deaths and 100,000 people became homeless.

The national and international support for the devastated area was enormous. As soon as possible, a start was made on the Delta Works, a system of dams and storm barriers which, together with the raising and strengthening of dykes, would make it impossible for something like the 1953 St. Ignatius Flood to happen again.

Although the Delta Works were officially completed in 1997, Holland remains locked in a constant fight against the water.

DUTCH SPECIALTIES

The Zeeland *babbelaar* (chatterbox) is often called the cheapest sweet in Zeeland. Every farmer's wife on Walcheren used to make it once a week. It contains water, sugar, butter and vinegar. Visitors would be served their first cup of coffee with sugar and with their second cup, they would be served a butter "chatterbox" because it was cheaper than sugar.

The name of the sweet is taken from the people who hung around for that second cup of coffee. They were real chatterboxes.

In 1892, confectioner J.B. Diesch started the production of butter chatterboxes. His recipe is still the foundation of the only genuine Zeeland butter chatterboxes sold to tourists in tins.

"A market is being held here. What stall is right at the beginning? French fries! They are always a hit."

French fries—deep-fried strips of potato—made their appearance in Holland at the start of the 20th century as a snack at fairs and festivals. They came from the Belgians, Holland's southern neighbors. Around 1912, the first French fry houses appeared in the red-light district of Rotterdam. In 1954, the first French fry business was opened in Amsterdam.

Today, French fries have a permanent place as a side dish or snack and they are sold in a paper cone or a plastic dish. The most popular order is *patat met*—French fries with mayonnaise.

Zeeland mussels are mussels that are processed, packaged or sold in Yerseke in Zeeland. The mussels can also be imported. In Holland, mussels are mainly bred in the Oosterschelde and the Wadden Sea. Pollution has reduced the natural population of mussels in the North Sea by around 70%. The mussel season runs from mid July to mid April. In Holland, mussels are usually steamed and eaten with bread and sauces or with French fries.

Dutch cheese is famous throughout the world and has been made since time immemorial. Dutch cheeses have travelled throughout the world since the middle ages. Annually, Holland produces 674,000 tons of cheese, some of which is exported to 130 countries. Since 2010, Gouda and Edam cheeses have been protected European brands—only cheeses actually produced in Gouda and Edam are allowed to use the names.

TILT AT THE RING

"In the Zeeland summer, they organize the traditional tilt-at-the-ring contests. Here they are practicing for it."

Tilt at the ring has several regional versions. In Zeeland, the sport is practiced by farmers who gallop bareback on a Zeeland shire horse along the ring track, holding a lance. They then try to skewer a ring with a diameter of 15 inches suspended halfway along the track. If the contest ends with two participants in a tie, additional rounds are held, each time with a smaller ring. The competitor who misses first is the loser.

The children stand in two rows opposite each other and take hold of the person standing opposite with arms crossed. During the first part of the song, they make a sawing movement with the arms. At "From your race, race, race," all the pairs except the first one let each other go and take a step backwards. The front pair skips through the path that has appeared. At the end of the song, they join the back of the line, so that the following two children can now be at the front and the song can start again.

GOOD HOPE Herman Heijermans (1864-1924) lived for a few years in Scheveningen and Katwijk aan Zee. He used the hard fisherman's life that he witnessed there in his play *Op hoop van zegen* (*The Good Hope*), about Kniertje, the wife of a fisherman, who loses her husband and two sons to the sea. Despite this, she sends her other two sons to sea where they drown. The play contains a famous sentence that has become a Dutch proverb: "The fish are dearly paid for." More than a century later, the play is still performed. It was filmed in 1986 by Guido Pieters.

FIGURE FROM CHILDREN'S LITERATURE

"An important cultural figure for Zeeland is Reynaert de Vos"

Van den vos Reynaerde (About Reynard the Fox) is a 13th century story, written in Diets (Middle Dutch) by a certain Willem—we don't know his last name. It is about the crafty fox Reynaert, who is far too clever for all the highly placed officials. It is an allegory on society, which presents the nobility as incompetent, the clergy as hypocritical, and the people as stupid and coarse.

Van den vos Reynaerde has been able to influence important foreign authors, because it was translated into Latin in 1278. Geoffrey Chaucer (1343-1400) used fragments in his famous *Canterbury Tales* and William Shakespeare (1564-1616) named the character Tybalt in *Romeo and Juliet* (1595-1596) after Tybeert the Tomcat. The story mentions the Zeeland town of Hulst where there is now a statue of Reynaert de Vos.

ARCHITECTURE

"There are Scottish houses in Veere because a real Scottish nobleman lived here. From 1444 onwards, there was a lively trade in sheep's wool from Scotland, which is a strange story. I drew the lamb next to the nobleman to indicate the wool trade."

In 1444, the Lord of Veere, Wolfert VI of Borsele, married the Scottish princess Mary Stewart. From that moment, Veere became the depot for sheep's wool from Scotland, and various Scottish merchants made their home in the city. A Scottish merchant lived in *De Struijs*, the Scottish House with an even house number. The name of the other house, *Het Lammeken* (The Lamb) recalls the wool trade. The Scottish Houses are now a regional museum with period rooms.

The Sikorsky S-51 was the first helicopter in Holland. It was sold to the Royal Navy, which gave it the name "Jezebel." Jezebel saved people from trees and roofs during the Flood and was decommissioned in 1959 after nearly 7.5 years of faithful service.

"The Flood of 1953 is the most recent flood of that scale, but in 1421 the St. Elisabeth Flood occurred. The same story."

In 1421, around the name day of St. Elisabeth (19 November), a storm flood hit Holland. The flood was probably not really that high, but the dykes were neglected and were breached in several places. The counties of Flanders, Zeeland, and Holland were largely submerged. 2,000 people lost their lives.

What is remarkable is that this is the second of three St. Elisabeth floods. Two other major floods took place around the same day in 1404 and 1424. Some of the repairs undertaken after the flood of 1421 were destroyed in 1424. At the moment, a decision was taken not to repair the Holland Waard, resulting in the creation of the water-rich natural area of the Biesbosch.

"There was often flooding in the past. That's why people built a sort of mounds where you could go if the water rose and so escape drowning."

The first refuge mounds date from the 11th century. They were only one or two yards high and offered room for one small farm building. In the centuries that followed, these artificial hills were raised to five and sometimes even twelve yards. People then used these mounds to build "motte-and-bailey castles" that were habitable observation towers. There were around 170 motte-and-bailey castles in Zeeland. Not a single one has survived, but there are around forty refuge mounds dotting the landscape.

THE FLOODS

ADVERTISING

"Somebody mentioned, 'In Zeeland, they won't like you only showing misery.' It is beautiful there as you can see by the advertising for Zeeland in the summer."

are now a regional museum with period rooms.

The Plompe Toren (the Plump Tower) is a tower that stands in an isolated landscape on the Oosterschelde. The tower is 75 feet high and dates from the 15th century. It was originally part of the church of the village of Kouderkerke. The village was destroyed before 1700 by the rising water of the Oosterschelde, but the tower survived. Today the renovated tower is a tourist attraction owned by the Association of Nature Monuments.

"You would think that this tower is from a church, but that isn't the case. This is the city hall."

Everaert Spoorwater (un-1474) designed the city hall of Veere (1474-1517). For centuries it served as town hall and court, and contained the town archives. Today, the building houses the Town Hall Museum "De Vierschaar," with a collection that includes historical portraits of the Orange monarchs. Veere has enjoyed a special bond with the Orange dynasty since 1581, when Willem of Orange was made Marquis of Veere. King Willem-Alexander is also Marquis of Veere. The tower has a carillon with 35 bells.

The Onze-Lieve-Vrouwe Church (Church of Our Lady) is also called the Great Church. It opened in 1521 as a Catholic church, filled with pomp and splendor. In 1543, the Bishop of Utrecht officially consecrated it to Saint Mary Major. Less than thirty years later, in 1572, Veere swore allegiance to the Prince of Orange, and the church became Protestant. All the church ornaments were sold and a wall was built between the nave and the transept.

Over the centuries, the church has endured much including fire and decay. In the French period, the nave was turned into a four-storey hospital. Towards the end of the 19th century, there were suggestions that the building should be demolished, but it was saved and became a national monument in 1890. The nave has been used for football matches, for a time it was a party venue, and during the flood, it was used to house cattle that had been rescued. In the 1970s, the church was designated for cultural use and since then exhibitions and concerts have been held there.

THE DELTA WORKS

In the Delta Works plan, the whole of the Oosterschelde was to be shut off by a dam. But in 1974, when three miles of a total of nearly six miles of the dam were completed, the work had to be stopped. If the Oosterschelde were completely dammed, it would mean that no more seawater could stream in. Fishermen were anxious about losing their livings and environmental organizations pointed out the consequences for the plant and wild life in the area. In 1976, the decision was finally taken to make sliding doors in the rest of the dam that could be closed in the event of storm or spring tide. When the storm barrier was opened in 1986, it turned out that this decision had made things much more expensive than budgeted.

"To be able to put Neeltje Jans in the book, I thought up a school."

Neeltje Jans was the name of a sand flat in the estuary of the Oosterschelde, named after a boat that had once run aground here. It is the Dutch name for the old Celtic-Teutonic patron saint of fishermen and sailors, Nehalennia. In 1970, the sand flat was raised in order to turn it into a work island for the construction of the Oosterschelde barrier. Today you can visit Delta Park Neeltje Jans and enjoy a day out with seals and sea lions, water attractions, and exhibitions about the Delta Works. There is a memorial plaque with the text, "Here go over the tide: the moon, the wind and us."

In 1965, Queen Juliana opened the Oosterschelde Bridge, which is more than three miles long, and links Noord-Beveland with Schouwen-Duiveland. When it was opened, it was the longest bridge in Europe. Two years after the opening, the bridge was renamed the Zeeland Bridge.

FIRST HALF OF FEBRUARY

FUN ON THE ICE

THE ELEVEN CITIES TOUR

As early as the 19th century there were men who would skate along the eleven cities of Friesland. In 1895, Pim Mulier was the first person to clock the time he took to complete the whole tour. In 1909, the first official Eleven Cities Tour was held and whoever finished the course was awarded an Eleven Cities Medal. Because of the changing climate, the tour could be held eleven times in the first fifty years, and only four times in the second fifty years. In 1985, women took part for the first time. That year saw the fastest time ever skated when Evert van Benthem completed the nearly 200 kilometres in 6 hours and 47 minutes.

FAMOUS DUTCH

"You can hardly see the Willem Drees Path anymore, because it's covered with snow. Willem Drees is part of Dutch history, but how can you illustrate that man for a child of today? Nobody knows what he looks like. My eighty-year-old mother remembers him, but the most a child will know is his law. That's why I did it like this, because then they can't say I forgot him."

C WILLEM DREES (1886-1988)

THE WELFARE STATE

Willem Drees was Prime Minister for ten years, from 1948 to 1958. Although he was a social democrat through and through, he was able to get the support of the parties to the right and left.

During his government, he made sure the decolonization of Indonesia went well, entered into an important agreement with the Americans which made the rebuilding of Holland possible, and ensured that the elderly and unemployed were insured for basic benefits. He meant so much for the country that they still speak of "Daddy Drees."

At the moment he resigned his position as Prime Minister, the queen appointed him Minister of State. That is an honorary title for an exceptional politician who can subsequently be consulted by the head of State.

Drees lived to the age of 101. He was able to enjoy the welfare state he built up for quite some time.

"In Franeker, you can visit the Planetarium."

C EISE EISINGA (1744-1828)
THE ENLIGHTENMENT IN HOLLAND

Eise Eisinga was a Frisian wool carder. He would comb sheep's wool into fine silver—a heavy but well-paid occupation. In his spare time, he studied mathematics and astronomy. In 1774, there was a Frisian preacher who claimed that the earth would leave its orbit and would burn in the sun because four planets would collide. To prove that this was impossible, Eisinga decided to build a moving planetarium. It was completed in 1781, and this planetarium shows the correct position of the planets even today. Eise Eisinga was a child of his time, as the 18th century is also known as the Age of Reason. The French ideas about the Enlightenment were adopted in Holland. The ideas began to blossom that science could lead to the discovery of truth, that religious truth need not necessarily be correct, and that leadership should be in the hand of people who were capable, rather than passed down from father to son.

"Holland has ice clubs. I mention the Jaap Eden Ice Club because Jaap Eden was a special person."

Jacobus Johannes Eden (1873-1925) won his first world title on skates at the age of 19. He topped the Adelskalender—the world rankings of all-round skating—for 2191 days. He also became world champion in cycling, but he squandered his prize money on his flamboyant lifestyle, and died as poor as a church mouse at the age of 51.

The first Dutch artificial 400-metre ice track is named after him. This opened in Amsterdam in 1961 and was the world's third artificial ice track.

TRADITIONAL COSTUMES

"Here's a chain of people arm in arm and we have various traditional costumes next to each other."

Today there are very few people who wear traditional costumes. Only the elderly wear the clothing every day and a small group wear the costumes for special occasions.

This is the traditional costume of Bunschoten-Spakenburg. A striking feature is the *kraplap* worn by the women, which is a broad shoulder piece with large, colorful flower print. When a woman is in mourning, she wears a plain, dark *kraplap* that is black, purple, or navy blue.

Traditional costume of Urk. The women wear a *kraplap* of colored silk with embroidered flowers or a tight bodice. During the week, the apron is made of striped material and on Sunday of black wool.

Traditional costume of Huizen. The Huizen traditional costume is the only one with the high white starched lace ear broach cap, which is worn over a white cotton under-cap. The rest of the costume is fairly somber.

Traditional costume of Staphorst. If a woman is not in mourning, she wears red. The mourning color, however, is worn a lot—white for four years if a parent, spouse or child dies; black with a plain blue cap for two years on the death of a grandparent, grandchild, or brother or sister; blue if somebody has died and the woman has received an invitation to the funeral.

Traditional costume of Groningen. A cap broach with golden filigree on other side is placed over two under-caps, one white and one black. A lace sloppy cap is worn over all this.

The colorful traditional costume of Hindeloopen is completely different to that worn in the rest of Holland. Fabrics brought to Holland from the Dutch East Indies by the voc are used including chintz, a cotton fabric painted with flowers, and East-Indian calico, a checked fabric. The long waisted jacket made from chintz is called a *wentke*. A married woman wears a clasped bag and a tall headdress, and an unmarried woman does not.

Traditional costume of Marken. Women from Marken make their own traditional costumes and decorate it with embroidery. They wear hardly any jewelry. The clothing is based on costumes from the 16th century. For special church occasions and on Christian festivals, they wear antique clothing belonging to the family.

Traditional costume of Zuid-Beveland. The Protestant woman wears her hair in a blis—a roll on her forehead. Golden crown pins attach the large shell-shaped lace cap to the under-cap. The woman wears five or six strands of red coral around her neck. The striking man's hat is known as a castor hat or *pluuz'n'oed*.

"What struck me is that the Volendam women have bare arms with a sleeve that only reaches to above the elbow. The other regions all have a winter costume, but the Volendammers don't have one even though they are always outside. They are really tough."

Traditional costume of Volendam. The Volendam traditional costume with the characteristic *hul*, the white cap, is so well known that internationally people think it is the national Dutch traditional costume.

Traditional costume of Twente. The lace goffered cap shows how rich a family is—the richer the family, the finer the pattern. The Sunday costume is known as *kistentuug* when women wear a black skirt over several petticoats and a black jacket except in the city of Enschede, where the Sunday jacket is colored.

FUN ON THE ICE

On a *prikslee*, you move yourself over the ice using sticks just like skiing. There are seat sledges that you propel with your feet and on some versions you can use your feet to steer. There is also the knee sledge where you can exert more force and move faster by kneeling down.

"The Dutch often skate in a group, sometimes with all of them holding on to a stick."

"The Dutch sail everywhere—on the water, on the beach, on the ice." In 1600, engineer Simon Stevin (1548-1620) had the idea that a cart could move faster if you put a sail on it. Prince Maurits of Nassau (later of Orange) (1567-1625) saw something in the idea and paid for its development. In 1602, the first sail cart raced at 30 mph over the beach. The ice yachts are based on this concept, as they are boats fitted with a broad beam with skates fitted to either end. The average speed of an ice yacht is 37 mph.

"This is what it looks like if I try to skate, because I simply can't get the hang of it."

"A family in Friesland asked me whether this grandma with the walker was their grandma. I answered, 'She is as of today.'"

"Performing capers on two wheels is very Dutch."

King Willem-Alexander, when he was still prince, proposed to his beloved Máxima on the frozen Court Lake in The Hague.

The open-air ice-skating track was named after the servant of the Germanic god Thor who was renowned for his speed. In 1986, the track was covered and was only the second indoor ice track in the world. Today, Thialf is ranked third on the list of the world's fastest ice tracks.

KLUNEN

Klunen is Frisian for walking on skates in places where there isn't any ice, such as when a tour on natural ice runs through certain places where the ice is too thin. Mats are placed on the banks and the skaters *klunen* over them to the place where they can skate further on the ice.

COAT OF ARMS

Although the image of the Frisian coat of arms had been known for centuries, it was not until 1897 that the Frisian flag was drawn by heraldic artist Heerke Wenning (1847-1903). He described it as follows: "In blue, three diagonal white stripes, and on them seven red water lily leaves, arranged two, three and two." It would take another sixty years before the States Provincial officially adopted the flag in 1957.

A klapskate has the blade connected to the front of the foot sole by a hinge. The other end of the blade is not attached to the shoe. This allows a skater to stretch his or her legs naturally, without sticking the point of the skate into the ice. The idea had already been registered in 1894, but the Dutch motion scientist Gerrit Jan van Ingen Schenau (1944-1998) developed it into a practical skate in 1980. The klapskate demanded a new skating technique. In 1996, the Dutch women's team started using the skates and two years later it was in use by all top skaters.

"On the ice, you can get cake and 'zopie.'"
Soope was the 17th century name for a hot drink of rum, bock beer, eggs, cinnamon, cloves, lemon, and sugar. Today, the *cake and zopie* stall mainly sells thick pea soup, hot chocolate (sometimes with rum), and *gevulde koeken*, cakes containing almond marzipan.

In 1907, a clock and sewing machine shop started importing bicycles and putting together their own bikes under the name of Batavus. The production quickly increased and the range was also extended over the years with sport cycles, family bikes, delivery bikes, etc. In 2001 and 2007, Batavus was awarded the prize for Bike of the Year.

THE PAINTINGS

The playing children can be found on two paintings by Pieter Bruegel the Elder (1525-1569), *Census in Bethlehem* (1566) and *Hunters in the snow* (1565).

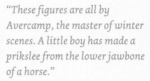

"These figures are all by Avercamp, the master of winter scenes. A little boy has made a prikslee from the lower jawbone of a horse."

"This lady with her bare bottom is not something I made up. It is by the painter Avercamp. He often painted people in less elegant poses such as pooping or peeing. This couple has fallen over, and in those days they didn't wear underpants. That's why they have bare bottoms."
Detail from Hendrick Avercamp (1585-1634), *Ice Scene Near a Brewery* (1610-1615)

The oldest jaw sledges are from the 13th century. A board was attached to a horse's jawbone, and the sledge was ready. This little boy on the sledge appears in the painting *River View With Skaters* (undated) by Hendrick Avercamp (1585-1634).

"I think this is a particularly beautiful fragment from a painting by Hieronymus Bosch."
Detail from the left panel of the Anthony triptych, or *The Temptation of St. Anthony* (c. 1501), by Hieronymus Bosch (c. 1450-1516)

Detail from *Winter Landscape* (1837) by Barend Cornelis Koekkoek (1803-1862)

NURSERY RHYME

Seven little frogs
Sat in a ditch
The ditch froze over
The frogs were half dead
They didn't breed, they didn't croak
From hunger and sorrow
Seven little frogs
Sat in a ditch

(text: Jan Pieter Heije [1809-1876], music: Joannes Josephus Viotta [1814-1859])

FIGURES FROM CHILDREN'S LITERATURE

Afke's tiental: een schets uit het Friesche arbeidersleven (*Afke's Ten: A Sketch From the Life of a Frisian Laborer*) was written by Nienke van Hichtum, the pseudonym of Sjoukje Troelstra-Bokma de Boer (1860-1939). The book appeared in 1903 with drawings by Cornelis Jetses (1873-1955).

"Carnival takes place in the second half of February. Both Limburg and Brabant are famous for their exuberant carnival celebrations. Because I had already drawn an illustration of Limburg, I chose Brabant for this, and Breda in particular. I went and joined in the carnival before drawing this. It was a very special experience. The people are incredibly good to each other—big, small, old, young, everybody is merry. They build floats and wear fancy outfits. The children also dress up and there is a children's parade. I asked whether the partygoers went home for dinner, but that wasn't the case. They only eat French fries and things like that—a good foundation for all that drinking that is part and parcel of carnival. I thought it was rather fun to have Superman ordering French fries! Robin Hood also wants some fries, but he'll have to wait his turn."

SECOND HALF OF FEBRUARY

CARNIVAL IN BREDA

BURGUNDIAN CARNIVAL

In Breda, they celebrate the Burgundian carnival along with the greater part of Northwest Brabant, Zeeland, and Gelderland. On the other hand, the Rhineland carnival is celebrated in Limburg and Northeast Brabant. For the Burgundian carnival, a Prince Carnival is chosen by each village, town, and city, who, assisted by eleven "councilors," is given "power" for four days. Traditionally, the mayor will give the Prince the keys to the city, symbolizing this change of power. During carnival, the village, town, or city is given a different name.

While the clothing for the Rhineland carnival cannot be crazy enough, the costumes for the Burgundian carnival used to be fairly simple. A classic costume is the peasant smock with a scarf. Today, however, a lot of work generally goes into the carnival costumes.

NURSERY RHYME

"The song is 'Hello Mister Owl' from The Fables Newspaper, but you could think of many others with all those carnival figures."

Hello Mister Owl
Where are you taking us?
To the land of Fables?
Ah yes, to the land of Fables
And will you read to us from the Fables Newspaper?
Yes, from the Fables Newspaper
For there you read
Exactly how the animals are
Really?
Yes, really
Really Mister Owl?
Mmm mmm...
For animals are exactly like people
With the same people wishes
And the same people tricks
And it's all in the newspaper of the Land of Fables
Land of Fables
The Fables Newspaper
And now
Cuddle up in your warm nests, and remember
Eyes shut and beaks closed.
Sleep well

The Fables Newspaper was a children's puppet series on television, based on an idea by screenwriter Leen Valkenier (1924-1996). Mister Owl read from *The Fables Newspaper*, so that everybody could follow what happened to the animals in the Land of Fables. Between 1968 and 1974, 1041 episodes were made, and they are still regularly rerun on television. The Dutch series was sold to more than forty countries throughout the world.

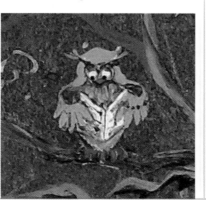

FIGURE FROM CHILDREN'S LITERATURE

"This is Dikkie Dik by Jet Boeke, a really nice lady."

Since 1977 Jet Boeke (1948) has written countless stories about Dikkie Dik. These were first intended as stories to be read out loud during the television series *Sesame Street*, but they quickly appeared in book form.

HORSES

"These jute horses are something from former times. They have been around for a very long time and appear in the parade every year."

DUTCH SPECIALTIES

C NAPOLEON BONAPARTE (1769-1821)
THE FRENCH PERIOD

The Dutch Republic had been ruled from 1795 by the French, when Napoleon Bonaparte made his brother Louis "King of Holland" in 1806. Louis, however, took the side of the Dutch against his brother, so in 1810, Napoleon removed Louis from the throne and took over himself.

Three years later, Holland was independent again, but in the intervening time Napoleon had ensured that a "registry of births, deaths and marriages" was introduced. From that moment, everybody in Holland had to have a last name. He introduced the meter as a measurement of length and kilo as a measurement of weight. He also introduced the "Napoleonic Code," a modern judicial system in which all subjects were equal before the law and justice took place in public.

HOT DOG

"A carnival fan sent me a photo of this costumed dog. With two fabric rolls and a fabric squirt of mustard you have a hot dog."

"Philips of course doesn't only make televisions so I have also shown an iron, a coffee machine and so on."

In 1891, father Frederick Philips (1830-1900) and son Gerard (1858-1942) founded the company Philips & Co in Eindhoven that began by manufacturing electric light bulbs. Within a few years, they were the largest in Europe and more technological products were added to the range. By 1932, Philips was the largest supplier of radio sets on the world.

Since 1914 it has had its own research laboratory, as an important part of the company. Major inventions include x-ray equipment, the audiocassette, the compact disc and, together with Sony, the DVD.

The *krakeling* is considered a genuine Dutch cookie, but it appears in other countries, too. In former times, the poor would pray with their arms crossed over their breasts, and this is thought to be the origin of the krakeling shape.

VINCENT VAN GOGH

C VINCENT VAN GOGH (1853-1890)
THE MODERN ARTIST

Vincent van Gogh started painting after he had been dismissed from his uncle's art shop. First he painted in Holland, including the famous *The Potato Eaters* from 1885. Later, he left for Paris where his brother Theo had an art gallery. There, he came into contact with colorful, experimental impressionism and Japanese prints. These influences were immediately visible in his paintings.

Vincent was an unhappy man whose love was never returned and had attacks of depression. In 1888, after an argument with his friend the painter Paul Gauguin, he cut off part of his ear. That is why there are a number of self-portraits with a bandage around his ear. He had himself admitted into a psychiatric hospital because he heard voices, and finally committed suicide. He was then just 37.

The only painting he ever sold while alive earned him 400 French francs. His *Portrait of Dr Gachet* (1890) was sold in 1990 for $82.5 million.

FINE ARTS

"Van Gogh didn't paint The Potato Eaters in Breda but rather in Nuenen. I thought he must have cooked a couple of potatoes and placed them on a dish so that he could let the whole potato feeling get through to him. Only then would he start painting."

Vincent van Gogh (1853-1890) working on his *The Potato Eaters* (1885).

TRADITIONS AND FESTIVALS

It is a Burgundian tradition to change the names of towns and villages during carnival. During carnival, Breda becomes Kielegat. The *kiel* in Kielegat refers to the farmer's smock that many people traditionally wear during carnival.

In former times, a guild was an association of people who practiced the same trade or shared the same interests.

The figure on the poster is a member of Guild of the Holy Sacrament of Niervaert. Around 1300, a consecrated host was found by peat cutters in the village of Niervaert, which began to bleed when anybody touched it. This Holy Host was taken to Breda and became the object of worship. The Guild of the Holy Sacrament of Niervaert was founded in 1463 to promote the worship of the consecrated host. Although the consecrated host was lost during the Iconoclastic Fury of 1566 and the guild remained dormant for a long time, the guild is currently making efforts to turn Breda into a place of pilgrimage, and it organizes the annual Niervaert procession.

HISTORY

C THE TELEVISION (from 1948)
THE BREAKTHROUGH OF A MASS MEDIUM

Television programs had been broadcast in Germany, England, and America since 1935. Technically speaking, the Eindhoven business Philips was fully geared for it, but the government obstructed things. They thought it too expensive and unnecessary, and the radio broadcasting companies also felt threatened.

That is why Philips started experimenting itself in 1948 with broadcasts from Eindhoven. In 1951, they covered the west of Holland where most people lived. From that moment, things developed very quickly. After ten years there were one million television sets in Holland for just twelve million Dutch. Each week, more than twenty hours of television were broadcast. By 1970, a tv could be found in almost every Dutch home. Thanks to the introduction of digital television at the end of the 1990s and television via satellite, thousands of international channels can be received in every living room.

"This is the home of a very chic family. Grandpa and grandma and their grandchildren Gerrit-Jan and Piet-Heintje have come to watch the carnival. Grandpa thinks it far beneath him and certainly won't take part. He concentrates on literature and the origins of the language, and that's why this poster is hanging here."

C HEBBAN OLLA VOGALA (c. 1100)
WRITTEN DUTCH

It was thought for a long time that the oldest Dutch words in writing were taken from a sentence scribbled down by a Flemish monk in order to try out his quill. "Hebban olla vogala nestas hagunnan hinase hic anda thu, wat unbidan we nu," — probably a sentence from a love song. It literally means, "All birds have started their nests except me and you, what are we beginning now?"

Now, many older fragments have been discovered. There is, for example, the baptismal oath of Utrecht from the end of the 8th century, which contains very understandable Dutch, "Gelobistu in got alamehtigan fadaer," *Geloof je in God (de) almachtige vader* (Do you believe in God, [the] almighty father").

The Dutch language began to develop in the 5th century from German. A book of legal code in Latin from the 6th century, the so-called *Lex Salica* (written between 509 and 511) contains recognizable Dutch explanations of Latin words including "hano" for *haan* (cockerel), "hengist" for *hengst* (stallion) and "fogal" for *vogel* (bird).

C THE CONSTITUTION (1848)
THE MOST IMPORTANT LAW OF A STATE

The first constitution, which regulated the balance of power in Holland, was introduced in 1798. It confirmed the constitutional entity of Holland, together with the freedom of religion and of the press. The constitution was amended several times over the years, but the king retained much of his power.

In the 19th century, citizens throughout Europe rebelled against the government, and King Willem II (1792-1849) gave Johan Rudolph Thorbecke (1798-1872) the task of designing a new constitution. The new constitution came into force in 1848. The citizens were given much more power and this included the election of the Lower Chamber and the States Provincial as well as freedom of education and association. The ministers were still appointed by the King, but they were responsible for their own policy. It is sometimes said that the introduction of this constitution marked the start of democracy in Holland.

The foundation of Thorbecke's constitution is still maintained today, even though much has been changed in the intervening period. In 1917, suffrage for men above the age of 23 was regulated, followed shortly thereafter by the right to vote for women. In 1971, the voting age was lowered to 18.

"Child labor actually did take place in the Dutch textile industry. These are very famous photos of children sewing. At the top, there is a little boy who spends all his time taking out loose strands of wool from a loom. That was extremely dangerous work. This factory building in Tilburg is now the Textile Museum."

C RESISTANCE TO CHILD LABOR (19th century)
OUT OF THE WORK SHOP, INTO SCHOOL

In the 19th century, it was perfectly normal for children to work. Their labor was needed on the land, in the store, or in the workshop, and many families could use the extra pennies. Around 1860, doctors and teachers began to protest, particularly against child labor in factories where unhealthy conditions were rampant.

Samuel van Houten (1837-1930), a member of the Lower Chamber, joined them in their objections and drew up a law. "Article 1: It is forbidden to employ or take into employment children below the age of twelve years." The "Children's Law" of Van Houten was adopted with 64 votes for and 6 against. From 1874, child labor in factories and workshops was forbidden, but children were still allowed to work on the land. This came to an end when compulsory education was introduced. From 1 January 1901, all children between the ages of 6 and 12 had to attend school.

THE FATHER OF THE FATHERLAND

"This illustration contains a lot of history including Willem van Oranje [Willem of Orange]. I couldn't really draw him because the most famous episode in his life is when he is murdered and that happened indoors. I found out that Breda has a Willem of Orange Boulevard. That was great. The Willem of Orange Boulevard is shut off so he is in the book."

C WILLEM OF ORANGE (1533-1584)
FROM REBELLIOUS NOBLEMAN TO "FATHER OF THE FATHERLAND"

Willem of Nassau was born in Germany. At the age of eleven, he inherited the Principality of Orange in Frankrijk, which explains his name, Willem of Orange-Nassau.

Through inheritance and his first marriage, Willem of Orange became count, marquis, lord and baron of countless places spread over the Netherlands. Thanks to this, he was one of the most important noblemen in Holland. His one great desire was to unite the seventeen Netherland provinces into one Republic under one government of nobles. Before he succeeded, Balthasar Gerards murdered him on 19 July 1584. He is nevertheless seen as the founder of the Republic that became a fact a few years later, and became known as the "father of the fatherland."

"This is the province of Overijssel that includes Kampen, Zwolle, and surroundings. In February, we celebrated carnival and now it is time for an early Easter. For the beginning of March, I have illustrated the Easter Festival of the believer. Later, in the second half of March, we will get to the business with Easter eggs."

FIRST HALF OF MARCH

EASTER IN OVERIJSSEL

HANSEATIC LEAGUE

"Kampen illustrated as a Hanze city."

C THE HANZE (1356-c. 1450)
MERCHANT CITIES IN THE LOW COUNTRIES

In the Middle Ages, a number of merchant cities worked together in order to operate more strongly. The Hanze, or Hanseatic League, as this alliance was called, began in Germany and was expanded with merchant cities in Holland, Belgium, Poland, Norway, Sweden, and the Baltic States. Cities in England, Russia, and Finland also belonged to the Hanze for a while.

The Hanze cities traded in the area of the Baltic Sea and the North Sea. Participation in the Hanze was voluntary. It had enormous advantages—travelling together was safer and the trading interests could be better defended in a large group. In Holland, the cities that joined the Hanze were mainly in the north and east. The power of the Hanze was enormous and its cities flourished. The wealth of these places can often still be seen in city walls, merchant houses, and other distinguished buildings.

In the end, the Dutch Hanze cities came off worse against the growing strength of the merchants in Holland and Zeeland.

"Here the Cog Ship that we saw on the illustration of the wadden islands returns. Kampen is the ship's homeport."

PEAT AND REED CUTTING

"Peat cutting used to take place in this region. Somebody explained to me that this part of Holland lay so low because for years they cut peat and this lowered the level of the land."

By cutting peat—a layer of old vegetation remains—from the ground and allowing it to dry, you ended up with turfs that make a first-rate fuel. The Romans were amazed that the Dutch were about to conjure up fire from the dried peat. Peat remained an important fuel until well into the 19th century. The peat layer was often several yards thick and as it was cut away over the centuries, many lakes and ponds were formed in Holland.

TRADITION

*"They say you see Abraham or Sarah when you reach the age of fifty. What do they do in Holland? They place a doll in the garden of the person celebrating their birthday. The French would never do that.
I've illustrated an Abraham and a Sarah together."*

In the Bible, the Jews say to Jesus: *"'You are not yet fifty years old,'* they said to him, *'and you have seen Abraham!'"* (John 8:57, NIV).

This statement is said by folk tradition to mean that anybody who turned fifty would see Abraham (or Sarah if you were a woman).
In some regions they bake "Abrahams" to celebrate the fiftieth birthday. These figures are bread or cake, decorated with spectacles, a pipe, a staff, and a beard of cotton wool. This custom became popular when Queen Juliana in 1959 and Prince Bernhard in 1961 were given such dolls on their fiftieth birthdays.

NURSERY RHYME

"'The song here is Kortjakje. She's walking with a book filled with silver work, a short skirt, and long legs."

Kortjakje is always ill
In the middle of the week, but not on Sunday
She goes to church on Sunday
With her book filled with silver work
Kortjakje is always ill
In the middle of the week, but not on Sunday

The Dutch text of the song is written to the melody of the French song "Ah! Vous dirai-je, maman" from the 18th century. In 1778, Mozart wrote twelve variations on the melody. Kortjakje was probably a girl of easy morals. Her short jacket (blouse) indicates that she doesn't pay much attention to etiquette. The suggestion that she was "ill" in the middle of the week could mean that she spent the best part of the week in bed, and finally went to church on Sunday to count her "silver work" or the money she had earned.

Reed cutting has also taken place since prehistoric times. There were houses in Holland with thatched roofs as early as 6000 BCE. Reed cutting is done in the winter season from mid-December to the end of March. After the reed is cut, it is sorted, cleaned, and bundled together to dry. Reed is still frequently used for roofs, and it is also processed in other products. In many places in Holland, reed cutting is a necessity because otherwise the rivers would become silted up.

EASTER

from bread dough to a wooden cross. They decorate the cross with chains of sweets, nuts, and fruits and with twigs and palm leaves. Carrying their palmpasen, they go along the houses, singing:

Pallem, pallem Pasen, Ei koerei!
In one Sunday we'll get an egg
One egg is no egg
Two eggs is half an egg
Three eggs is an Easter egg!

In 1870, the Matthew Passion written by Johann Sebastian Bach (1685-1750) in 1727 was performed in Holland for the first time. Thanks in part to Willem Mengelberg (1871-1951) and the Dutch Bach Association (founded in 1921), the performance of the work at Easter has grown into a tradition. Today, there are more than a hundred performances of the Matthew Passion (or arrangements of it) every year. The most famous has been presented in the Great Church in Naarden since 1922, and is attended by many Dutch celebrities and members of the government.

The triptych on this poster is by Rogier van der Weyden (c. 1400-1464), the painter in the tradition of the Flemish Primitives who, together with Jan van Eyck (1390-1441), is considered the most important Dutch painter of the 15th century.

In Denekamp, a *boaken*, a stake, is built before Easter. On Easter Sunday, a large group of people under the leadership of two chosen men—Judas and Iscariot—go to the castle Huis Singraven to ask the lord of the castle for an Easter stake. Then the allocated fir tree in the grounds of the estate is cut down and dragged to the *boaken*, accompanied by a long line of people. The branches are removed and the Easter stake is placed next to the *boaken*. A barrel of tar is suspended at the top. In the evening, both the *boaken* and the barrel of tar are set on fire. The tree that ultimately remains standing is auctioned off by Judas to those present.

"This is Ootmarsum. At Easter, they take part in vlöggeln.*"*
Vlöggeln has been a tradition since at least 1840 and is carried out by eight Roman Catholic bachelors who do not plan to marry in the coming four years. They are called the *Poaskearls* (Easter chaps). Once they have walked around the stake on a hill outside Ootmarum, the *Poaskearls* go hand in hand, followed by the people of Ootmarsum and the tourists, in a long chain to the center of the town. Singing Easter songs, they walk going straight through homes and cafés (where the *Poaskearls* are offered a drink) to the market square. There, any children are lifted into the air three times, to symbolize the resurrection of Jesus. This ritual takes place on both Easter Sunday and Monday. On Easter Sunday, the Easter fire is lit in the evening.

On Palm Sunday, the Sunday before Easter, children make a palmpasen by fastening an orange and a cockerel made

---

DUTCH SPECIALTIES

"Deventer is also one of the Hanze cities. They bake Deventer Cake there."
Deventer is also known as the "Cake City." The recipe for Deventer Cake has been a strictly held secret since the start of the 15th century. Deventer cake bakers have joined together in a guild where the secret is guarded. Only quality cooks were allowed to use the city eagle as their logo. They were sold in Hanseatic League cities as far away as Norway. In 1593, Jacob Bussink founded his bakery "In de van oudsher gekroonde Allemansgading" (Traditionally rewarded by everybody), and concentrated on the produc-

tion of Deventer Cake. Other companies came and went but Bussink has survived and Deventer Cake from Jb. Bussink is still considered the only genuine article.

"Union on fait force" ("Unity engenders power") was the text which bike traders Van den Berg saw on a boat. They decided to call their bicycle company Union. First, the brothers imported bicy-

cles, but from 1911 they started manufacturing themselves and even gave cycling lessons because bikes were not that common. The one millionth Union bike was produced in 1966. Ten years later, disaster struck when, in 1976, the bicycle factory was burnt to the ground. They managed to rebuild the company, and at the start of the 1990s, they acquired several other factories. Union was itself taken over by the Dutch Bicycle Group in 2005, but the brand still exists and new models are still regularly introduced.

In 1952, Wehkamp's Factory Office in Slagharen began a mail order company where people ordered articles they had seen in advertisements in magazines, and the postal office delivered the items to the purchaser's home. In 1985, Wehkamp was part of

the London-based The Great Universal Stores and the telephone computer allowed people to place their orders around the clock. Ten years later, the first steps were taken on the Internet, and in 1999, the complete range, now some 10,000 articles, could be ordered from the website.
In 2006, the company once again came into Dutch hands. In 2008, the last paper catalogue was published because the online store had taken over. Wehkamp.nl, as the company was renamed, now supplies some 163,000 articles per year and handles around five million shipments.

In 1952, L. Ten Cate bv was founded in Twente. The company specialized in underwear and was the first company to sell seamless hose imported from the

United States in Holland. Today the company makes underwear for men, women, and children. It has also developed the lingerie and fragrance line TC Wow with former top model Daphne Deckers (1968). They have introduced swimwear under the name of Tweka and also work with the brand Lief! on colorful underwear and pajamas for children.

A *moorkop* (chocolate éclair) should not be confused with a Bossche Bol (see p. 28). The choux pastry of the moorkop is lighter than that used for a Bossche Bol, and the top of a moorkop should have a blob of cream, possibly crowned with a slice of pineapple or a segment of tangerine.

BLUE FINGERS

"The people of Zwolle are called 'blue fingers' because they earned the name in a quarrel with the people from Kampen. Zwolle had sold its carillon to Kampen, but when it arrived, the bells turned out to be damaged. The people from Zwolle, however, still wanted their money. The people of Kampen thought, 'We'll pay you back—literally!' They collected the money owed in change from the townspeople and took it to Zwolle in carts. There, the copper change had to be counted by hand causing the blue fingers. 'Blue fingers' was originally a derogatory term word for people from Zwolle. Today they are proud of that name."

There are other stories about how the people of Zwolle got their nickname. Some say it is a reference to the treason of Zwolle against the bishop of Utrecht. First they had sworn allegiance to the Bishop, with two raised fingers. Later, they welcomed his enemy, the Duke of Gelre. Anybody who committed perjury was called a 'blue finger.' Today, the Zwolle's annual Blue Finger Days is a four-day market with a large number of events.

KLOOTSCHIETEN

"In Overijssel they practice a sport known as klootschieten. I couldn't draw it clearly so I thought I'd put it in a panel."
Klootschieten is based on the same principle as the shot put—a lead-filled ball (the *kloot*) must be thrown as far as possible. There are various types of courses and balls of various weights and sizes. The first *klootschiet* course was constructed at the end of the 14th century. The sport was particularly popular around 1500.

ECLLESTIASTILAL HOLLAND

C THE ICONOCLASTIC FURY (1566)
THE CONFLICT BETWEEN RELIGIONS

In the middle of the 16th century, dissatisfaction grew among the Dutch population. Nobles were angry because the Spanish rulers were usurping more of their power, the common people suffered from poverty and unemployment, and a growing group of Protestants wanted to follow their own faith when only Catholicism was permitted.

In 1566, the smoldering burst into flame. Nobles complained at the estate of Margaretha of Parma, but their words fell on deaf ears. Worse, they were called *Geuzen*, Beggars. From that moment, the rebellious nobles took the name Beggars for themselves.

During a secret service of Protestants in Steenvoorde, a clergyman called on them to destroy the Catholic churches. The violent action spread to other cities. All classes of the population took part. Within three months, the interior of Catholic churches and institutions throughout Holland were completely destroyed.

The Spanish king sent the Duke of Alva to Holland to restore order. Alva took strict measures and many Protestants fled abroad. Willem of Orange was among them and from Germany he organized the resistance to the Spanish rule that would lead to the Eighty Years' War.

Because the Protestants were not allowed to profess their faith openly in Spanish Holland, secret services took place in the open air in 1566. These services were called *hagenpreken* or hedge sermons.

"This signpost stood in a square in Ommen. For the Calvin Church, turn right. For the Dutch Reformed Church, turn left. The Roman Catholic Church, straight ahead. The Hong Kong Restaurant is that way. This is as Dutch as you can get!"

The 250-foot high "Pepper box" or Our Lady's Tower in Zwolle was built between 1454 and 1463. The tower is part of the The Assumption of Our Lady Basilica. In 1590, Catholic services were forbidden. From that moment, the building was put to all sorts of uses—circus tent, shooting range, refuge for the homeless, you name it—anything but church. It was not until 1809 that King Louis Napoleon returned the basilica to the Catholics and the church was restored.

Initially, the top of the tower was flat. It was only in the 18th century that an onion-shaped dome was placed on the roof. The present roof dates from 1815 and was put into place following a fire in the uppermost part of the tower.

"The Catholics are entering their church, and the stricter worshipers, recognizable from their hats and long skirts, walk in the opposite direction."
Converted Reformed believers have strict dress codes. Based on the conviction that there are differences between man and woman and that those differences should also be expressed in clothing, it is appreciated if women have long hair, wear a skirt at a length that does not cause offence, and that they cover their heads during services. Men should dress neatly and properly and they must remove their headgear during the service. This is in accordance with 1 Corinthians 11:6-7: "For if a woman does not cover her head, she might as well have her hair cut off; but if it is a disgrace for a woman to have her hair cut off or her head shaved, then she should cover her head. A man ought not to cover his head, since he is the image and glory of God; but woman is the glory of man." (NIV)

BASSIE AND ADRIAAN

"Bassie and Adriaan in a car."
The brothers Bastiaan (1935) and Adriaan van Toor (1942) have been playing the clown Bassie and the acrobat Adriaan since 1978. For more than 25 years, TV shows have featured the incredibly popular duo having exciting adventures and performing in the circus.

Since 2003, Bassie has been appearing as a solo act. Very occasionally, Adriaan still appears in his role as acrobat, but generally he stays in the background. The duo also appears as characters in an animation series.

GIETHOORN

"This is Giethoorn and it was quite a job to work out how the bridges and roads are arranged there. There are bridges that lead to somebody's house and are not intended for public use. There are also bridges, which the public may cross so that you may continue on the other side."

The network of canals and ditches in Giethoorn arose to enable the transport of peat. Giethoorn is sometimes called "Holland's Venice." The only through road is a bicycle and pedestrian walkway. Otherwise, all transport takes place by water, mainly with punts, which are small flat-bottoms that are propelled forward with a pole, just like a gondola.

"The farm buildings in Giethoorn are often built on a mound, which you don't find anywhere else."
The hump in the thatched farmhouses arose because the lower front house was attached in a makeshift way to the much higher hay barn. The barns were so large because hay was the most important source of income.

"This floating brass band is in honor of Bert Haanstra, who used such a boat with a brass band in one of his films."
Film director Bert Haanstra (1916-1997) filmed his light-hearted

Fanfare (1958) about a brass band, which, as a result of a disagreement, split into two competing groups in Giethoorn. There is a monument in memory of Haanstra and his film in the village.

TRADITIONAL COSTUME

"This is Staphorst. I went there long ago, and a lot of children were walking around in traditional costume. It was beautiful. This time I was very disappointed because not a single child was dressed like that. The only ones who wear the traditional costumes are very old ladies."

ARCHITECTURE

"Here again is a Dutch lift bridge, one of the many types of bridges in this country."

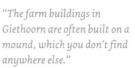

"Here, I've shown a scene from the Middle Ages, just for a bit of fun."

"A turf hut, or sod house, was sunk half way into the ground. It wasn't easy to live in one. This one is in the Open Air Museum."
In the turf areas, a house was allowed to remain standing if it was built in one night between sunset and sunrise and the chimney was smoking in the morning. A turf hut, also known in Dutch as a *spitkeet*—did not have any walls because the living area was dug out of the ground. The roof was covered with heath turfs. It was housing for the very poor, and because of the damp, the cold, and the vermin, they didn't survive very long.
In 1901, living in a turf hut was forbidden.

"This is a bakery. In the Middle Ages, fire could flare up quickly because so many buildings were built of wood. The house where you could bake your bread was therefore located some distance away. This bakery is actually in the Open Air Museum in Arnhem."

Castle Rechteren near Dalfsen is the only medieval castle still standing in Overijssel. It has belonged to the same family since 1315 although it has been occupied on several occasions in that time, including Spanish troops in the 16th century and Munster troops in the 17th century. The castle is not open to visitors, but there is a legend of a haunted room, the door to which has been kept shut for centuries since a rabid huntsman was locked in.

The traditional colors of a Staphorst farm building have a special meaning—the shutters and doors are green, symbol of the young life of nature, and white, the color of purity. The blue color on the lower edge and the windowsills is added to ward off evil. The roofs used to be made of straw, but since the 1940s, reeds have been used.

"I wanted to include a zoo in the book for the children. Since we are now in Drenthe, I immediately thought of the zoo in Emmen. Yet, it is a pity for the others if I only showed one zoo so that's why I've made a compilation.

Drenthe has megalithic graves. I thought it would be fun to show a prehistoric village. Back then, a megalithic grave looked completely different to the ones we have today. The stones that we recognize as a megalithic grave used to be covered with turf so it was nothing more than a mound with some stones around it. I thought that was a pity so I've drawn both a prehistoric farm building with such a mound and a farm building from the 17th century, next to a megalithic grave such as those we know today."

SECOND HALF OF MARCH

DRENTHE AND THE ZOO

DRENTHE IN PREHISTORIC TIMES

"This is a megalithic grave in prehistoric times: covered with earth and grass."

C MEGALITHIC GRAVES (ca. 3000 BC)
THE GRAVES OF THE FIRST INHABITANTS

There are 52 megalithic graves in Drenthe. The piled up stones are the graves of the first inhabitants of Holland and date from around 5,000 years ago.

There is no way of stating for certain how the stones were moved, but probably tree trunks were used to roll the stones —sometimes weighing up to 22 tons—to the desired spot. The ground beneath the stones was dug out and the dead were placed there. Because the dead were given grave gifts—objects they had used during their lives—we know more about the life of the first Dutch people. They were hunters who, after they had spent some time roaming, took up residence in peat farmhouses. They worked the ground with wooden and stone tools and kept their food provisions in pots.

There are also two megalithic graves in Groningen.

"Here is a megalithic grave, like the ones you now see in Drenthe."

"A prehistoric girl, known as Yde girl, was found in this area. Her face has been reconstructed."

In 1897, two peat workers found the preserved body of a girl, who had been killed 2,000 years ago. A band around her neck and a wound near her collarbone suggested that she was sacrificed or had received the death penalty for some offence.

Studies showed that the girl was approximately 16 years old and five feet tall. Her back was crooked and she probably had a limp. The girl's face was reconstructed.

The peat workers stated that they had found the girl near Yde. It later turned out that they had lied and they had been working illegally in the Stijfveen when they found the body. Afraid of being caught, they said she had been near Yde. That is why the bog body has gone down in history as "Yde girl."

Yde girl can be seen in the Drents Museum that is housed in the old province house of Drenthe (1854) in Assen.

NURSERY RHYME

I saw two bears buttering bread
Oh it was a wonder!
It was a really wonderful wonder
That the bears could butter their bread
Hi hi hi, ha ha ha
I stood and watched them do it

This old lie text—where the text is clearly untrue— has countless variations, such as **"I saw two monkeys harvesting wheat;" "I saw two fleas folding caps"** and **"I saw two cats matting chairs."**

"Patterson Pepps is in Artis."

The first verse of the song "Dikkertje Dap" (Patterson Pepps) dating from 1950 by Annie M.G. Schmidt (1911-1995) goes:

Patterson Pepps climbed up the steps
With a sugar cube from the table
And the giraffe came out of his stable
"Hi, Giraffe," said Patterson Pepps
"D'you know what Mommy gave me?
Bright red boots for when it's rainy!"
"Can it be true?" said the giraffe
"Patterson, Patterson, what a laugh."

Translated by David Colmer

ZOO

OUWEHANDS ZOO

"In Rhenen there is a park for mistreated bears that were found in Yugoslavia and other countries where they make bears do tricks. In this park, the animals can develop a proper bear existence. The first time I visited it, I saw two bears that had become friends who walked around with their coats touching each other.
I discovered that bears walk in patterns. The paths you see were not thought up by me, but were worn out by the bears that kept taking the same route. Apparently, bears are also brought here who have never been around water. In the beginning they don't understand it at all, but at a certain moment they realize, 'Hey, this is nice!' Then they simply go a sit in the water for a long time—it's wonderful to watch. They also go and lie on a tree trunk and let their legs dangle as well as relax their muzzle and meditate."

The Bear Wood is only one part of Ouwehands Zoo.
In 1919, Cor Ouwehand opened a chicken farm, and a lot of people went there to look at the birds. In the depression years, Ouwehand grew into a real zoo. The television series ZOOP, which was shown on Nickelodeon for six years in the 2000s, was shot here. There were also three films with the same name. The RTL program *Jungle Club* was also shot in Ouwehands Zoo.

APENHEUL

"The Apenheul Primate Park is also worthwhile. The lemurs walk around free—it's really cool."
Photographer Wim Mager (1940-2008) bought two pygmy monkeys from a pet shop, which ignited his passion. Finally, Mager gave up his job and started the Apenheul Primate Park in Apeldoorn, a place where monkeys and apes do not sit around in cages but can move freely in large outside runs. The park began with monkeys in 1971 and introduced gorillas five years later. Over the years, the number of species has grown. Where possible, the animals roam free. Where that is not possible, the animals and people are separated as unobtrusively as possible.

DOLFINARIUM

"In the Dolfinarium, there are special mornings where children who need extra care, can participate in dolphin therapy that helps them make learn how to interact with other people."
The Dolfinarium in Harderwijk, which opened in 1965, is the largest sea mammal park in Europe and houses dolphins but also sea lions, porpoises, seals and wal-

ruses. You can walk around in the park to view the animals, as well as visit various shows featuring the sea creatures.

AMERSFOORT ZOO

In 1948, the Amersfoort Zoo started with a number of children's farm animals, as well as a monkey, a camel and a black bear. It grew into a zoo with no fewer than 1,500 different animal species, a Dino Wood, and playgrounds.

BLIJDORP ZOO

"Rotterdam is here with Bokito, the escaped gorilla, of course. That's a great story."
Blijdorp Zoo in Rotterdam began as a bird garden. In 1857, The "Rotterdam Zoo" was opened, but only members—prominent citizens of Rotterdam—were allowed inside. In the depression years of 1930s, the zoo moved to the Blijdorp district. By then, non-members were also allowed to enter the park.
During the bombing of Rotterdam in the Second World War, the zoo was badly hit. Many animals were killed, a zebra fled into a shopping street, and seals swam around in the city canals. But that same year, the zoo re-opened and from then on the park continued to grow.
Today, Blijdorp is arranged by world region so that animals, plants and cultural elements from the same regions are displayed together.

In 2007, the silverback gorilla Bokito jumped over the canal that separated him from the visitors and attacked a woman who visited him four days a week. The incident introduced a new word in Dutch: *Bokitoproof*, "proof against breakouts."

BURGERS' ZOO

Burgers' Zoo in Arnhem opened in 1913. The zoo grew from a pheasant park into the most visited attraction in Gelderland. It was the first zoo that introduced accommodation without bars for the beasts of prey.
The zoo has various "eco-displays"—accommodations that mirror as closely as possible the natural living environment of the animals. These include Burgers' Safari, Burgers' Bush, Burgers' Mangrove, Burgers' Desert, Burgers' Ocean, and Burgers' Rimba.

EMMEN ZOO

Willem Oosting (1906-1983) founded Emmen Zoo in 1935. In the Second World War, Jews and members of the resistance hid there.
Today they call the zoo an EXPERIENCE park, and it is divided into various worlds of Icy Cold, Damp Warmth and Hot Dryness.

NATURA ARTIS MAGISTRA

"Now we see Artis. There's a little girl pushing a pram containing Artis de Partis."

Artis de Partis is the mascot of the zoo in Amsterdam: Natura Artis Magistra, or Artis for short. It is the oldest zoo in Holland.
In 1838 bookshop owner Gerardus Westerman (1807-1890) and two others took the initiative to open a zoo in Amsterdam. Westerman was the first director. Concerts were also given and a museum was founded, with the idea of "promoting the knowledge of Natural History in a pleasant and illustrative way." The importance of the zoo is shown by the fact that Artis received the first telephone connection in Holland.
Artis has since grown into a zoo that houses around 900 animal species and more than 200 varieties of trees.

Artist Erna Kuik (1967) wrote and illustrated *Twee lange oren* (*Two Long Ears*) in 2008. It tells the story of Bastiaan Haas (Bastian Hare).

"Ik bid nie veur bruune boon'n" ("I will not say grace for brown beans") is the famous exclamation of Bartje Bartels in the book Bartje (1935) by Anne de Vries (1904-1964).

The stories of the rebellious young boy in a poor laborer's family in Drenthe, and its sequel *Bartje Seeks Happiness* (1940), were incredibly popular. In 1972, a television series was made from the books. Since then, Bartje has become a symbol for Drenthe.

Suze Boschma-Berkhout made the stone statue of Bartje in 1954. In 1982, they made a bronze version. The statue is constantly "kidnapped" by New Year's associations.

TRADITIONS AND FESTIVALS

"Here I've shown the access road to the highway, because you have to take this exit to get to Assen. During the Easter season, the TT is held in Assen. All the motorbikes you see here are going there."

The *Tourist Trophy* (TT) of Assen is an annual motorbike race that is held on the TT Circuit Assen (or the Circuit of Drenthe).

In 1925, the Motorclub Assen en Omstreken (Bike Club of Assen and Region, founded in 1922), organized the first TT. Until 1954, the race took place on the roads. A closed course has been used since 1955. In common with all such courses, each bend in the Circuit of Drenthe has a name. Some bends are named after nature areas in the region, such as "Duikersloot" and "Meeuwenmeer." The "Ramshoek" is in honor of when sheep and rams grazed in this area of the Drenthe heath. "Ossenbroeken" was the place where farmers from the region fattened their bulls. The "Mandeveen" bend refers to the right-of-way by which farmers from Witten and Assen take several carts of turfs from the "shared peat."

"The non-religious Easter is all about eggs. I have hidden eggs everywhere in this illustration and there are thirty in all. That should keep the children busy for a while."

For the ancient Teutons, eggs were the symbol of fertility and new life. After the cold winter, the chickens started laying again, meaning that eggs could be eaten.

The earliest Christians saw eggs as a symbol of the resurrection of Jesus. The shell of an egg looks like a tombstone from which a living creature emerges. These Christians painted the eggs red at Easter, the color of the blood that was shed at Jesus' crucifixion. During fasting, people were not allowed to eat any eggs. They collected all the eggs the chickens laid during those forty days. In order to keep them edible, they were boiled or preserved in some other way. At Easter, when the period of fasting was over, there were quite a few eggs to eat!

The Easter Bunny is also a survivor of old Teutonic fertility rites. Via these Teutonic traditions, he has become part of Easter celebrations throughout the world.

From 1 March, countless Frisians go out looking for the first lapwing egg as the symbol for the start of spring. Traditionally, the first lapwing egg was presented to the Head of State. Today it is presented to the King's Commissioner in Friesland.

Although collecting lapwing eggs is forbidden in the European Union, Friesland has negotiated an exemption. Annually, a limited number of eggs may be collected, 5,939 in total, but no more than fifteen per person. Permission must be asked for each egg before it may be collected.

At the horse market in Zuidlaren, which is held every year in October, horses and ponies are sold in the traditional "hand clapping" way—the seller mentions a price, the buyer claps the seller's hand and says a lower price, the seller claps the hand of the buyer and suggests a higher price. And this goes on, back and forth, until one of the parties shakes the hand of the other, which means he agrees and the sale is sealed.

MEANDER

"Here runs the Aa, a river that winds attractively through the landscape."

"People in Drenthe often place stones to mark off their territory. They are found in the ground there."

c. 140,000 years ago, during the Saalian Glacial Stage, the driving force of the ice pushed large stones from the north to Holland. We call these stones "traveled boulders." Drenthe is particularly is full of them.

CLOWN

Pipo the Clown was thought up by scenario writer Wim Meuldijk (1922-2007). Actor Cor Witschge (1925-1991) played the clown in almost 700 television episodes, which travelled the world in a caravan with his wife Mammaloe and his daughter Petra.

TOADS

From February to April, toads migrate from their winter home to the water to reproduce. Along the edge of the roads that the toads have to cross, toad protectors dig buckets into the ground. Regularly they take out the toads that have fallen into the buckets and put them on the other side of the road, so that they can safely continue their journey.

The roof is a striking feature of authentic farm buildings in Drenthe. These are partly tiled and partly thatched because tiles were originally more expensive for roofing than reed. The more tiles a farmer had on his roof, the richer he was.

Saxon farm buildings have traditional blue-white-black shutters. The thatch is made of rye. In the spring, you can see how well the farmer has threshed the rye because if the rye has been badly threshed it will start sprouting.

This is a farm building from the Iron Age (from c. 800 BCE). There were living quarters and an area for the animals all under one roof. The walls were from wood and wickerwork, and were covered with turfs of straw and loam. The roof was made from wood, heather, reed, or straw.

DINO'S

"The zoo in Amersfoort also has a prehistoric section. If you want to know how big a dinosaur was, you must certainly pay it a visit. I have to admit it is a bit creepy but children love it.
Incidentally, this book contains one dinosaur that isn't actually in the park. It is an allosaurus, which I found in a toyshop."
Dinosaurs from different periods are all walking around here together.

During the Jurassic—150 million years ago—you could run into:
- Euoplocephalus: 20-foot long herbivore
- Stegosaurus: 30-foot long herbivore
- Brachiosaurus: 75-foot long herbivore
- Allosaurus: 42-foot long carnivore
- Diplodocus: 80-foot long herbivore

In the late Cretaceous period—75 million years ago—you would see:
- Styracosaurus: 18-foot long herbivore
- Oviraptor: 5-foot long herbivore
- Triceratops: 30-foot long herbivore
- Tyrannosaurus rex: 45-foot long carnivore
- Pachycephalosaurus: 18-foot long herbivore

A meteor probably hit the earth nearly 66 million years ago and caused the extinction of the dinosaurs.

DUTCH SPECIALTIES

In 1753, Egbert Douwes and his wife opened a shop in Joure specializing in colonial articles. Their son Douwe Egberts later came to work in the business and ensured that the articles, including coffee, tea, tobacco and candy were sold far outside Joure. Yet it took until 1919 for a second branch to be opened in Utrecht. In 1960, the Douwe Egberts company was responsible for more than half of the national coffee and tobacco exports. In 2001, Douwe Egberts—which had in the meantime been acquired by the American Sara Lee—developed the Senseo coffee machine that works with pads, with Philips. It conquered the world in no time. Since 2012, Douwe Egberts is once again independent, under the name of D.E. Master Blenders 1753. Brands such as Kanis & Gunnink, Van Nelle, Moccona, Pickwick, and Coffee Company are all part of DE.

The company Knorr specializes in dried and concentrated products with a long shelf life. The company was founded in 1838 by Carl Heinrich Knorr (1800-1875) and came to Holland in 1957. Knorr

is now part of Unilever, an Anglo-Dutch company in the field of food products, personal care and cleaning articles. Within Unilever, Knorr is the brand that generates the highest turnover.

You will find the history of Vroom & Dreesmann on p. 45.

"They love to eat apple syrup in Holland."
At the beginning of our era, the Teutons were already making apple syrup by boiling apples until they turned into syrup that could be kept for a long time. The high sugar and iron content makes it a much-loved sandwich topping today.

"The Dutch love thick pancakes with heavy toppings because

you can enjoy them for days afterwards."
Restaurants specializing in pancakes can be found mainly in Holland and Belgium. Pancakes are made with a batter of flour (originally half buckwheat, half flour), egg, milk, and a pinch of salt. They are eaten with both sweet and savory toppings. The classic pancake is spread with sugar syrup and rolled up.

Dutch families used to bake their own bread. The first bakeries only appeared in the Middle Ages. In 1857, Doctor Samuel Sarphati (1813-1866) started the first bread factory in Amsterdam. The idea behind his Company for Flour and Bread Factories was to produce bread cheaply and to combat poverty. Thanks to a production of 9,000 loaves of bread per week, he could sell his bread for thirty percent under the price charged by the baker. Within eight years there were eleven bread factories in Holland.

"As we leave March, color returns to our lives. In April, we visit the bulb fields. They are behind the coast on North Holland as well as in South Holland. The bulbs include tulips, hyacinths, and daffodils."

FIRST HALF OF APRIL

THE BULB FIELDS

The first tulip bulb in Holland came from Turkey. Carolus Clusius (1526-1609), a doctor and botanist, planted the first bulb in the Hortus Botanicus in Leiden at the end of the 16th century.

The bulbs were incredibly expensive but much loved. In the 1630s, the tulip fever broke out. People were prepared to pay ridiculous amounts for tulip bulbs—sometimes as much as ten years' salary for a single bulb. Often, all they bought was a piece of paper stating that they were the owner of a tulip bulb that was still in the ground while in reality they owned nothing. There were people who thought the plague epidemic that broke out in Amsterdam (1633-1634) was a punishment for the ridiculous trade in bulbs. In 1637, this market collapsed.

In the 17th and 18th century, very rich people planted tulips in the gardens of their country estate in order to show off. In the 19th century, it became popular to grow the bulbs yourself. This meant that the bulbs became cheaper. Holland has specialized itself to such an extent in the cultivation of bulbs that today 65% of the worldwide bulb production and 75% of the bulb trade takes place in or via Holland.

THE FIRST CAR AND THE FIRST TRAIN

"Here you see the Spyker, the very first Dutch manufactured car. My father had one just like it. Do you like it? This is for my father."

Coachbuilders Hendrik-Jan and Jacobus Spijker—who also built the famous Golden Coach (see p. 29)—put together parts of German Benz cars in Holland. The result was the first Dutch motorcar, the Spyker-Benz. In 1903, the brothers changed the name to Spyker and built their own first model, which became the first car in the world with six cylinders and four-wheel drive.

In 1907, a Spyker came in second in the race from Beijing to Paris. Hendrik-Jan Spijker drowned that year, and Jacobus left the company, but Spykers continued to be built. In 1909, Spyker built the first ambulance and in the First World War, the company produced fighter planes. In 1926, the company closed, unable to keep up with the foreign competition.

"The topic of history can be found top left where you will see the first steam train. It traveled from Amsterdam to Haarlem in 1839."

⧈ THE FIRST RAILWAY (1839)
THE ACCELERATION

On 20 September 1839, the steam train De Arend ran from Haarlem to Amsterdam with a top speed just over 20 mph. The trip took 25 minutes. The line was extended to Rotterdam. Five years later, the route from Amsterdam to Utrecht was opened. By 1900, a complete rail network existed in Holland, run by various railway companies, and the train had become the most important means of transport for people and goods. The train made an important contribution to the industrialization of Holland.

In 1938, the existing railway companies joined together as the independent company Nederlandse Spoorwegen bv (NS—Dutch Railways), the shares of which all belonged to the state. Since 2003, the track has been managed by ProRail and the NS carries out the transport over the track, and everything to do with it. There is also a small number of railway companies that operate regionally.

The Dutch railway network is the busiest in Europe.

ARCHITECTURE

"If the bulbs have sold well, the growers build themselves beautiful houses. They make a mound on which the house is built with a beautiful gate at the front and an entrance to the fields at the

side. If you ask me, they never open the gate and always use the side entrance to the fields. The houses have many bay windows, columns, and so on and are quite special."

"What I noticed was that the bulb growers lay out their front gardens—squares and other angular shapes—in the same way as the fields."

"Of course, you have lots of greenhouses. I thought a nar-

row strip would be enough for showing the greenhouses. I could fill it all up, but there's nothing much else to see."

The first greenhouses were built way back in 1850. Vulnerable plant species could then be grown in this sheltered environment. The first greenhouses were filled with grape vines. Later they were used for all sorts of flowers, vegetables, and fruit.

The largest concentration of greenhouse cultivation in the world is in the Westland and around Aalsmeer. Around 10,000 hectares of greenhouses are operated by 9,000 companies. The greenhouses require lots of energy for heating. The greenhouse cultivation uses by far the most energy within the market gardening sector. Thanks to improving technology, it is possible to supply the generated energy to the electricity network on a growing scale.

FLOWER PAGEANT OF THE BULB REGION

"When I went to look at the bulb fields, two little girls were selling bunches of tulips. We immediately bought two bunches."

"In first part of April, there is a parade of floats made completely of flowers."
In April the annual Flower Pageant of the Bulb Region is held. The parade goes from Noorwijk aan Zee to Haarlem. This pageant is the only one that is made from bulb flowers.

The first bulb pageant took place in 1947, when an amaryllis grower from Hillegom, Willem van Warmenhoven, made a whale from daffodils on a small truck. All the bulb villages joined in and the pageant became bigger and bigger. Today, large floats, often decorated around a specific theme, parade past a crowd of visitors who come from far and wide to enjoy the colorful festival.

"The flowers grow in lines. These men are tracking down sick ones. They use a stick to remove the flowers that don't look natural, for a flower disease can put the whole harvest in danger."
Tracking down sick flower bulbs has been done since the start of the 20th century by so-called "sick seekers." They keep their eyes open for discolored leaves and strange growths, and remove the sick bulbs from the field with a "snitch" which is an iron tube. They wear special leggings to ensure that they do not spread disease through the fields.

KEUKENHOF

"This is where you can find the Keukenhof. Tourists and Dutch people visit it."
From the end of March until the end of May, the Keukenhof garden in Lisse is a showplace with more than seven million flowers from bulbs grown in the region. The estate of Castle Keukenhof (Kitchen Court) is also used for exhibitions and tours.
Keukenhof opened in 1950 and was the brainchild of the Mayor of Lisse and a number of bulb growers. Today, the flower garden, which is supplied by more than ninety growers, is one of the largest tourist attractions in Europe—75% of the 800,000 annual visitors come from abroad.

FloraHolland

"There is a flower auction in Aalsmeer. They're famous for that in Holland."
The flower auction Bloemenlust (Flower Pleasure) was founded in Aalsmeer at the end of 1911. Several days later, in 1912, the Central Aalsmeer Auction followed. It was a great success and in 1918, the Central Auction achieved an annual turnover of one million guilders. In 1968, both auctions merged and went further under the name Flower Auction Aalsmeer. After various expansions, it merged in 2008 with FloraHolland (which was in turn formed by combining several regional auctions). The logo of the Aalsmeer flower auction was retained.
FloraHolland, with Aalsmeer as the main branch, is now the largest auction for cut flowers and plants in the world. The annual turnover is more than four billion euro.

ENJOY

"The bulb fields are surrounded by frontage roads, where lots of campers park. The owners sit by their RV on a camp stool and enjoy a cup of coffee while gazing over the blooming fields."

NURSERY RHYME

Tiny little toddler
What are you doing in my garden?
You're picking all the flowers
And really messing things up
Oh my dear lovely mommy
Please don't tell daddy
I really will be good and go to school
And leave the flowers where they are

FIGURE FROM CHILDREN'S BOOKS

"This is Rupert Bear who is actually not Dutch at all, but he's so at home here that I've included him anyway."
Rupert Bear is the main character in the cartoon of the same name by Mary Tourtel (1874-1948). It first saw the light of day in the Daily Express. In 1935 Alfred Bestall (1892-1986) took over devising and illustrating the adventures of Rupert until 1965.

PENSIONERS

"What's so very amusing about Dutch people is that when they reach retirement age, they all buy the same bike—quality matters—and while they're out, they pick up a unisex windbreaker from the ANWB with the same color pattern."

CUTTING

"We love the flowers, but they are not good for the bulbs

themselves. That's why special cutting machines cut off all the flowers. At least, that's what I've been told."

"In the second half of April, King's Day, the nicest party in Holland, takes place. Somebody who lives on Marken said to me, 'You have to celebrate it with us, because it's a real party here on Marken. Just you wait and see. We've even got special outfits for the day.' On Marken, they traditionally collect the children from school across the dyke with the brass band. Lots of women play in it. Then they all walk together to the village square where they solemnly sing the 'Wilhelmus,' the Dutch national anthem. They then sing the traditional song of Marken and set off to party.

Queen Beatrix was still the monarch when I drew this illustration. Somebody asked me, 'What are you doing with the Queen? Just you see—she'll hand things over to her son just when the book comes out.' So I thought, 'I'll just paint them all—all the kings and queens that have ever ruled in Holland.' Fortunately, there are not that many: Willem I, Willem II, Willem III, Emma, Wilhelmina, Juliana, Beatrix and her son with his wife. I've depicted the old monarchs as paintings, because otherwise people may think it's a costumed ball. It's good that I solved it like that, because on 28 January 2013, Queen Beatrix announced her abdication and Willem-Alexander became King on 30 April. I have divided the illustration into two. On the left, the king is celebrating King's Day with his family. On the right, it's the people's King's Day."

KING'S DAY   27 APRIL

THE ROYAL FAMILY

C KING WILLEM I (1772-1843)
THE KINGDOM OF HOLLAND AND BELGIUM

In 1813, when the French were driven out, the son of stadtholder Willem V became the first king of Holland. He was King Willem I. He was given the nickname "king-merchant" because he concentrated mainly on repairing the economy. In South Holland, products had to be made that would then have to be sold throughout the world by the North Hollanders. Valuable goods also came from the colonies. The Catholic Belgium did not accept the Protestant king. The son of Willem I, Willem II took the side of the Belgian separation movement that declared the independence of Belgium in 1830. It would take until 1839 before Willem I recognized the independence. He was so disappointed that he abdicated the throne in 1840.

King Willem II (1792-1849)

Willem Frederik George Lodewijk succeeded his father in 1840. It was a tumultuous period in Europe. In February 1848, a revolution broke out in France, and the upheavals spread to Germany, Hungary and Italy. The large cities in Holland also began to revolt so Willem II set up a state commission in March 1848 under the leadership of Johan Thorbecke (1798-1872) to prepare a revision of the constitution. In 1848, he approved Thorbecke's new liberal constitution. He died not long after he had addressed the Lower Chamber.

King Willem III (1817-1890)

Willem Alexander Paul Frederik Lodewijk almost did not become king. He initially renounced the throne because he was angry that his father had approved the new constitution in which the king was stripped of much of power. However, he quickly reversed his decision and was king of Holland from 1849 until his death. Willem III was not an easy man. The older he got, the more unreasonable he became. Everyone around him knew that, so when he gave the order to place the mayor of the Hague in front of a firing squad because he did not like his behavior, everybody ignored him. Thanks to his irrational behavior, Willem III acquired the nickname of King Gorilla, yet the people respected him. When he became ill in 1888, he became more and more confused. That is why his wife Emma—who was 41 years younger than he—was appointed Regent on 20 November 1890. Willem III died three days later.

Regent Emma (1858-1934)

The three sons Willem III had during his first marriage all died before their father. He had one other child, a daughter, Wilhelmina, by his second wife Emma. Because Wilhelmina was only ten years old when her father died, her mother, Adelheid Emma Wilhelmina Theresia, acted as regent until Wilhelmina's eighteenth birthday. Emma was a descendant of the house of Orange-Nassau. Her father and mother were both great-grandchildren of Princess Carolina of Orange-Nassau and Prince Karel Christiaan of Nassau-Weilburg. At the age of twenty, she married the 61-year-old Willem III. After the death of her husband, she made a point of speaking to each minister every two weeks. In the eight years that she acted as Regent, she had to manage three cabinet formations. In addition, she prepared her daughter to become Queen of Holland on her eighteenth birthday.

Queen Wilhelmina (1880-1962)

Wilhelmina Helena Pauline Maria was installed as Queen six days after her eighteenth birthday on 6 September 1898. In 1901, she married Hendrik of Mecklenburg-Schwerin (1876-1934). She shared two great grandparents with her husband: Tsar Paul I and Maria Fjodorovna. In 1909, she had a daughter and named her Juliana.

In November 1918, Wilhelmina was able to restore calm when Dutch socialists under the leadership of Pieter Jelles Troelstra (1860-1930) tried to incite a revolution.

During the World War II, Wilhelmina headed the Dutch government in exile, and addressed her people via Radio Orange, a station forbidden by the Germans. Her speeches provided great support to many of her subjects. After the war, Wilhelmina lived in an ordinary house to show the people that she sympathized with them. She often rode a bicycle. Wilhelmina would have liked to see a change in Dutch politics after the war with more power for the crown, less sectarianism in politics, and a greater unity in the country. Neither the ministers nor the people, however, were eager for these innovations. In 1948, Wilhelmina handed over the monarchy to her only daughter, Juliana.

she was particularly interested in social issues. During her monarchy, she had to deal with no fewer than ten Prime Ministers. After she abdicated in 1980, Juliana no longer wanted to be called "Queen" but rather "Princess." She hardly ever appeared in public from 1995 until her death in 2004.

Queen Juliana (1909-2004)

Juliana Louise Emma Marie Wilhelmina married Bernhard van Lippe-Biesterfeld (1911-2004). They had four daughters: Beatrix, Irene, Margriet, and Christina. In 1947 and 1948, Juliana acted on two occasions as Regent for her mother. She was then involved in her first cabinet formation. On 4 September 1948, she was installed as Queen.

Juliana was a much more casual Queen than her mother. She wanted to be addressed as "Madam." The way in which she visited Zeeland in her Wellington boots after the Flood of 1953 to comfort the people was characteristic of her. If Juliana had been born into a commoner's family, she once said, she would have wanted to become a social worker. It is therefore hardly surprising that at her weekly meetings with the Prime Minister

"Beatrix seen from behind, with hat."

Queen Beatrix (1938)

Beatrix Wilhelmina Armgard would not have become queen if her parents had had a son after her. Only in 1983 was it legislated that the monarchy should pass to the oldest child instead of to the oldest son.

In 1996, Beatrix married Claus von Amsberg (1926-2002). The German Claus was able to win the sympathy of the people, partly by learning to speak Dutch quickly and by joining in the traditional Nijmegen Four-day March in 1967. The couple had three sons: Willem-Alexander, Johan Friso, and Constantijn.

Beatrix ascended the throne in 1980. On the day of her installation, Amsterdam became the scene of a battle between demonstrating squatters ("no

home, no crown") and the mobile police forces.

Beatrix was a more formal, business-like queen than her mother. She sharpened the protocol and wished to be addressed as "majesty." Her speeches were characterized by personal statements that sometimes conflicted with what the government would have liked to hear at that moment. Her political knowledge was extensive, but at a certain point, people felt that she involved herself too much in the formation of new cabinets. In 2012 a majority in the Lower Chamber decided that the Queen would subsequently play no role in the formation of the cabinet.

In January 2013, the then nearly 75-year-old Beatrix abdicated because the responsibility for the country should, she felt, be in hands of a younger generation. Beatrix is a lover of visual arts, in particularly modern art.

"The King with his beloved wife."

King Willem-Alexander (1967) and Queen Máxima (1971)

Willem-Alexander Claus George Ferdinand was the first male heir to the throne in 116 years. He studied history in Leiden, earned his pilot's license with the Royal Army and specialized in water management.

Willem-Alexander became popular thanks to his "ordinariness". He skated the Eleven Cities Tour, ran the New York Marathon and enthusiastically attended the events featuring Dutch athletes during various Olympic Games. From 1998 until he ascended the throne, he was a member of the International Olympic Committee.

In 2001, Willem-Alexander became engaged to the Argentinian Máxima Zorreguieta. From the first moment she was introduced to the Dutch people, Máxima became a public favorite.

On 02/02/02 Willem-Alexander and Máxima were married. The couple has three daughters: Amalia, Alexia, and Ariane. Willem-Alexander was installed as King of the Netherlands on 30 April 2013. Máxima became Queen at the same time. Willem-Alexander holds the following titles: King of

the Netherlands; Marquis of Veere and Vlissingen; Count of Katzenelnbogen, Vianden, Diez, Spiegelberg, Buren, Leerdam and Culemborg; Viscount of Antwerp; Baron of Breda, Diest, Beilstein, the city of Grave, the Land of Cuijk, IJsselstein, Cranendonck, Eindhoven, Liesveld, Herstald, Waasten, Arlay and Nozeroy; Master of Ameland; Lord of Borculo, Bredevoort, Lichtenvoorde, Loo, Geertruidenberg, Klundert, Zevenbergen, Hooge and Lage Zwaluwe, Naaldwijk, Planen, Sint-Maartensdijk, Soest, Baarn, Ter Eem, Willemstad, Steenbergen, Montfort, St. Vith, Bütgenbach, Niervaart, Daasburg, Turnhout and Besançon.

THE REPUBLIC AND THE PATRIOTS

"Two windows on history: the Republic and the Patriots. I thought this would be a nice contrast to King's Day."

C THE REPUBLIC

(1588-1795)

CONSTITUTIONALLY UNIQUE

In the Spanish war, the seven northern Holland provinces fought under Willem of Orange against the rule of the Spanish King Philip II. Holland was divided in 1588: the south became the Spanish Netherlands and the north the

Free Republic of the Seven United Netherlands.

It was never the intention to found a Republic, but there were simply no good options for king so they chose to form a government in which all seven regions would have an equal vote in state affairs. At the head of the republic were a Grand Pensionary (a sort of Prime Minister) and a stadtholder who also commanded the army. The stadtholder was often a descendant of Willem of Orange. It was not until 1648, at the

Peace of Munster, that the Republic was recognized as a sovereign state. It remained in existence until 1795, more than 200 years.

C THE PATRIOTS

(1780-1795)

CRISIS IN THE REPUBLIC

Things were not going well for the Republic in the 1780s. It became clear that England had surpassed the Republic in both trade and in international politics. Unemployment grew.

A group of citizens blamed

stadtholder Willem V for the misery. They called themselves patriots. They tried to expel Willem V with armed "volunteers."

Initially, Willem V enjoyed the support of the King of Prussia, but when the French came to the help of the patriots, the Republic fell in 1795. It was renamed the Batavian Republic, based on the example of the French Republic.

TRADITIONAL DUTCH CHILDREN'S GAMES

"On King's Day, they also play traditional games such as pooping nails, which is one I'd never heard of."

In **pooping nails** the participants get a rope or belt around their waists. On the back, there's a string with a nail knotted to it. The aim is for you to let the nail slip into the neck of a bottle without using your hands.

"Another Dutch game is: shuffleboard."

A **shuffleboard** is a wooden box that is about six feet in length. At the end of the box there are four gates with a point value written above each gate. The player is given thirty flat round wooden discs and must try to slide as many as possible through the gates in order to earn as many points as possible.

In **can throwing**, empty cans are built into a tower. Three balls are thrown from a certain distance, with the aim of knocking over as many cans as possible.

Stilts are two stakes with foot supports at the same height.
In **stilt walking**, the aim is to stand on the foot supports and walk by lifting the stakes one after another. The best way of doing that is to clamp the stakes under your armpits and hold the stilts at hip height.

In **sack racing**, the children have a jute sack in which they stand. Then they have to move a certain distance as quickly as possible. The fastest one wins.

For **bite the cake**, slices of gingerbread are hung up on string. With their hands behind their back, two (or more) children stand next to each other and try to eat the cake as quickly as possible.

In **Pin the tail to the Donkey**, a child is blindfolded and tries to attach a tail with a thumbtack to the right place on a picture of a donkey.

THE FREE MARKET

"Here the people are celebrating with a traditional free market. This is typically Dutch—anybody can get their old junk from the attic and sell it. Children enjoy doing it. Often they also play an instrument to collect money. Somebody plays an accordion, a little boy plays the drums, and I have another one playing the flute. They also think up games—as long as they can earn money.
There is a lot of music, people enjoy themselves and in the end, when the party is over, the whole street is littered with rubbish, but it's always such a lot of fun."

Queen's Day or King's Day has been held in Holland since 1891 Traditionally, vendors did not need a permit for selling their goods on that day. That custom has grown into the free market.

"The Dutch wear all sorts of orange things on King's Day including sweaters, trousers, caps, and even wigs. They put on inflatable plastic crowns or wear enormous glasses with orange frames."

"Here are two boys I met at the time. One of them is crying, because his father told him to

play and he didn't really want to. Because he was crying, everybody gave him money and the boy next to him didn't get anything. That was amusing. I gave them both some change."*

"Pick and choose is also typically Dutch. 'Either 2.50 each or five euros for two.' As long as they have the idea of getting a bargain.
Free is really great. The Dutch will come out of their house for that, even if it's something dirty or ugly. As long as it's free, they've got to have it."

"There are children who think up little tricks to earn money. This little boy has made a bed and got into it, with a sign, 'I'll grow rich while I'm asleep.' Lie and wait, perhaps people will give him some money."

FIGURE FROM CHILDREN'S LITERATURE

"Jubelientje is the creation of Hans Hagen and the very gifted illustrator Philip Hopman."
Jubelientje (Jubilata) is the main character in the series of books of the same name, the first of which appeared in 1991. The books were written by Hans Hagen (1955) and illustrated by Philip Hopman (1961).

FIVE SUNFLOWERS

"Somebody is very pleased here, because he has just bought a Van Gogh for a euro."
Vincent van Gogh made a number of paintings of sunflowers. This is *Vase With Twelve Sunflowers*, the painting that he made in January 1889 and that now is worth tens of millions of dollars.

COPS ON BIKES

"Everybody cycles in Holland. There are even bike cops."

MARKEN

"This is the brass band in traditional Marken costume with additional orange especially for King's Day."

"The children in Marken also wear traditional clothing on King's Day. These suits have been in the family for generations. The very small boys wear a skirt, and as they get a bit bigger, they are given trousers that reach to just under the knee. People who are not born in Marken are often called 'long trousers.'"

"They make special fabrics in Marken that are used for traditional costumes. The curtains in front of the windows hang like a sheet to half-way down the window. They open that window to allow light to fall in, and on the lower part they hang little flags, also made from that traditional fabric. That's magnificent."

"Both swifts and swallows make their nests in Marken. Both breeds have their own territory."
The bird on the left is a swallow, the one on the right a swift.

These houses are on Marken. Marken used to be occasionally flooded, so that's why there is nothing in the garden except grass. The stakes are intended for the washing— washing can be clamped to the twisted rope attached to the stake.

The lower parts of the houses used to be open so that the sea could flow under it. Now they have bricked up those lower sections, but that is why all the houses have steps. The houses are detached and the land around them is public property. I know somebody who lives there in a detached house and you can walk all around it."

Marken used to be an island in the Zuiderzee. In 1957, it was connected to the mainland by a bridge. The water around it is now called the Markermeer. Since 1891, there has been a plan to drain the southwestern part of the Ijsselmeer where Marken is located. This would create the Markerwaard, but the plan was abandoned in 2003.

"This is the old town hall of Marken, which was for sale when I was there. I thought, 'I have to have a mayor, because the king is coming to celebrate.'"

THE ZAANSE SCHANS

Old buildings from the Zaan region are collected on the Zaanse Schans. Between 1961 and 1974, the historical houses and windows were literally moved here to give people an idea of how people lived in the Zaan region in the 17th and 18th century.

It is not really a museum because people actually live in the houses. Only a few houses are open to the public. The Schaan attracts more than 900,000 tourists a year.

"This is the first Albert Heijn. In reality, the building is much longer, but it's really about the front. It is still a shop."

The Albert Heijn museum shop opened on the Zaanse Schans in 1967. It is a replica of the grocery shop that Albert Heijn (1865-1945) took over from his father in 1887, and from which the mega chain of supermarkets with his name arose.

"This is a fisherman's house where Tsar Peter the Great once stayed. He wanted to earn his license as ship's carpenter and came to Holland to learn the trade. *He succeeded. He only stayed for a short time in this house, for it attracted so much attention that he decided to move elsewhere. The fisherman's house still exists though another building has been built around it to protect it. It is completely made of wood and inside the walls are filled with signatures. Over the years, it has become a place of pilgrimage for Russians. You cannot only find the signature of Napoleon on the wood, but also of Putin."*

Peter the Great, or Peter I Alexejevitsj Romanov (1672-1725), spent eight nights in 1697 in the Tsar Peter House, a laborer's house that was built from old ships' wood. He rented half the house of Gerrit Kist, a blacksmith's apprentice from Zaan who had worked in Moscow. It is one of the oldest wooden houses still standing in Holland.

ORGAN-GRINDER

In 1875, the blind Belgian Leon Warnies started a rental business for small street barrel organs in Amsterdam. This made him the founder of the barrel organ tradition that is still alive in Holland. The Warnies company was continued as Perlee. The barrel organs of G. Perlee are inextricably connected to Amsterdam. The large barrel organs today are almost all operated by an engine. After a period of neglect, smaller barrel organs are now again in favor.

"These are two buildings from Volendam. They do not have any special costumes for King's Day there, but wear their usual traditional costume."

"This house is in Broek op Langedijk, which largely has wealthy Amsterdammers as residents. The houses there are all gray, in all sorts of shades; it is exceptionally beautiful. It appears very distinguished, but it had its origins in poverty. The houses were of wood, so they had to be painted, otherwise the water in the vicinity could damage them. Yet, there was no money for a special color. That's why the village residents mixed all their leftover paint with white, and this became the gray color we now find so attractive."

DUTCH SPECIALTIES

"They also bake orange cakes On King's Day. This woman thought, 'I'll put on an orange dress and pop into my friend's for a cup of tea.' She has already laid out the cakes, but the cat, whom the lady is scared of, is eating them."

For King's Day, bakers make orange versions of all different types of cakes. Here we see *moorkoppen*: cream éclairs covered with orange chocolate.

"These four friends aren't selling things on the street; they're off to eat cakes together."

The *tompoes*—cream slice—is a Dutch cake that was thought up in the 19th century by a confectioner in Amsterdam, which is a layer of patisserie cream between two layers of puff pastry. The top is covered in a pink glaze. On 27 April, cream slices are sold with an orange glaze.

There are also whipped cream slices, where there is whipped cream instead of patisserie cream between the slices of puff pastry.

Zaandam houses the Verkade factory. In 1886, Ericus Gerardus Verkade opened his steam, bread, and rusk factory De Ruyter. He began with the production of bread, rusks, honey gingerbread, and cinnamon rusks, called *langetjes*. Later, Verkade began specializing in cake and chocolate. In 1950, the company was given the distinction of "Royal."

Verkade was one of the first companies to employ women. This gave rise to the expression "the girls of Verkade"—hundreds of unmarried Amsterdam girls who travelled every day to the factory in Zaandam to work. Today, the expression is again being used in advertising. The girls of Verkade today are women who enjoy life, love, and Verkade biscuits.

The mustard seeds for Zaans mustard have been ground in windmill De Huisman on the Zaanse Schans since 1961. Zaans mustard is, in common with most Dutch mustard, coarse mustard containing the husks of the mustard seed. Zaans mustard is available in three varieties: coarsely ground, finely ground and coarsely ground with broken pepper.

Jantje Beton (Jantje Concrete) is a national youth fund that has collected money since 1968 to pay for provisions for children. The name refers to the encroaching blocks of apartments (beton = concrete) against which Jantje rebels. He makes it clear that thought must be given to providing special play areas for children. Queen Beatrix made the statue of Jantje Beton based on a drawing by Robert Bouwman.

KERMIS

"I didn't have any room, unfortunately, for the fun fair, so I made a panel here. From here you can go to nearby Amsterdam."

There is traditionally a fun fair in Amsterdam on the Dam around King's Day.

NATIONAL ANTHEM

"There are several songs to be found in this illustration, but the most important is the Wilhelmus. I think that's right for King's Day. There are more of them, but you'll have to look for them."

First verse:
Wilhelmus of Nassouwe
Am I, of German blood
Faithful to the fatherland
I remain to the death
A Prince of Orange
Am I, still unafraid
The King of Spain
I have always honored

The complete text of the national anthem has fifteen verses. The text in Dutch is an acrostic with the first letters of each verse forming the words "Willem van Nassov." The song is dedicated to Willem of Orange, the father of the fatherland.

The Wilhelmus was written between 1568 and 1572 to the melody of a satirical song against the Huguenots. It was only officially registered as the national anthem of Holland in 1932. When the kingdom was founded, the Wilhelmus was not considered suitable, partly because the Belgians may have found it too Calvinist. A song by the poet Hendrik Tollens (1780-1856) was chosen as national anthem ("Wien Neerlands bloed in de aders vloeit, van vreemde smetten vrij" [Who Ne'erland's blood feel nobly flow, from foreign tainture free]), but it didn't catch on, while the Wilhelmus gained in popularity from the north.

"Holland is divided into two. A question you often hear is, 'Do you live above or below the rivers?' To begin with, I didn't understand that at all, but it all becomes clear when you look at the map. The Lek and Waal Rivers flow from Germany to the North Sea and cut the country in half horizontally.
I started bottom left, in the Biesbosch. The really beautiful swamp-like natural area that is far more beautiful than I can draw it. It is located below Rotterdam. You can sail through it on a whisper boat, as well as paddle around and I don't know what else. It's highly recommended in May. It's really beautiful—there are flowers everywhere, the grass is incredibly high and the willows are starting to put out shoots.
Above the river, we go to the middle of the country, with the Betuwe, and the famous Kinderdijk is right in the distance."

THE RIVER REGION

THE BIESBOSCH

until his boat was full. It was heavy work and it took him several days. He delivered his load to the boss, who would then make quite a bit of money with it.
The withies came to the Biesbosch around 1800. Today, the cultivation of willows is done with machinery.

"In days past, you had the Biesbosch withies. They stayed for a week or two, because they had to travel from far away. The people stayed in houses they built themselves from twigs that were without any hygiene and really filthy. Apparently, a king paid them a visit and said that they couldn't live like this anymore. Then they built boats with houses on them that were a bit more comfortable and much better so the withies could relax a little."
A withy-bed is a swampy area where all sorts of willows grow. A withy would cut root suckers from these willows

"The twigs that the withies harvested from the willows were used to make chairs, baskets, and other things. It was a very important product for the economy."

"You have duck decoys in the Biesbosch. To attract the ducks, they put out duck models that float around."
The first duck decoy was registered in Holland in 1300. At the time, the ducks were caught for food. Today there are still a number of duck decoys in use—to create a hiding place for ducks and other birds, and to capture them for further study.

DODENHERDENKING EN BEVRIJDINGSDAG

"A piece of the Biesbosch was unoccupied territory during World War II. The Germans couldn't find their way. There were people in the resistance who knew the area like the back of their hand, and they helped refugees over the river into the Biesbosch.
This is the monument to these people. May 4 is the national Memorial Day and the flags hang at half-mast."
The men, who helped people to flee from occupied to liberated territory via the Biesbosch after 6 November 1944, were called 'line-crossers.' After the war, 21 line-crossers were commemorated. The monument illustrated here

called The Line-crosser is in Werkendam and was unveiled in 1989. It was designed by Niek van Leest (1930-2012).

"On May 5, they celebrate the Liberation of Holland. On that day in 1945, the Americans and Canadians drove through Holland with their jeeps. There are a lot of photos of young men and young women all happily waving flags. In those days, they all wore socks. That's fun.
In Canada, where my brother lives, I once met a woman who turned out to be one of those young women with socks. She married a Canadian soldier and has never been back to Holland. She wanted to speak a bit of Dutch."

DUTCH SPECIALTIES

The Betuwe is known for fruit cultivation because old riverbed is the best agricultural land in Holland. Fruit cultivation has developed rapidly in Holland since around 1875. Today, around 620 million kilograms of fruit are produced every year, with a value of $430 million. That is by no means enough to feed the Dutch population, because they eat more than one billion kilograms of fruit each year—an average of 132 pounds per person. Of all the fruit grown in Holland—of which 95% are apples and pears—more than half is exported.

Apples are the most popular among fruit growers in Holland. Annually, around 400 million

kilograms are harvested. Of these, 40% is exported.

Pear production is increasing rapidly in Holland. At the moment, around 200 million kilograms are picked. No less than 80% of these are sold abroad.

In 1904, the first Dutch fruit auction was opened, the "Auction of Geldermalsen and surroundings," and initially limited to cherries. In Holland, around five million kilograms of cherries are grown every year.

"Little summer kings" is the loving nickname given to Dutch strawberries. Around half of the strawberries grown in Holland are intended for export.

"This truck belongs to Vos, an enormous transport company. I do not know any of the people, but I once heard the owner on the radio say that when he was on the road, he always counted how many trucks he met from his own company. I really had to include it."

Harry Vos began a messenger service between Oss and Nijmegen in 1944 with just one car. During the post-war reconstruction, the

demand for transport grew and Vos stepped in. In 1998, the name of the family business was changed to Vos Logistics. Today, the company has thirty branches throughout Europe and employs almost 1,900 people. It operates around 1,200 trucks.

"I showed the asparagus fields in Limburg. This truck stood there doing nothing, because asparagus doesn't grow in November. Now it's busy in the middle of the asparagus season delivering the white gold."

ON THE WATER

"When we visited the river region, I said to my other half, 'I want to go on a ferry.' That costs € 1.50, a small amount for such a nice attraction. We went there on one ferry and came back on the next."

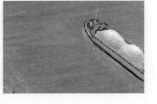

A "whisper" boat has an electric motor, which makes hardly any noise. They are the only boats allowed in many nature areas, because they do not disturb the peace and quiet.

In a bulk ship or bulk carrier, the goods for transport are tipped in bulk into the hold. If the goods are not impervious to water, the hold is shut at the top with large shutters. There are bulk carriers in all sorts of sizes, varying from a mini-bulker with a load bearing capacity of less than 10,000 tons to a VLBC (Very Large Bulk Carrier) with a load bearing capacity of more than 200,000 tons. Around 35% of all boats in the world are bulk carriers.

VIKINGS

"This is Dorestad near Wijk bij Duurstede. The place no longer exists. The Vikings came there across the water to pillage. They succeeded.
I have painted a number of children here, but they run away and hide so they'll be fine."

Dorestad was one of the most important trading junctions in Western Europe from the 7th until the middle of the 9th century. The Vikings heard of the wealth of the city and, between 834 and 863, they regularly plundered Dorestad. They murdered, enslaved the inhabitants, and took with them anything they could carry. The inhabitants grew quite used to this and simply rebuilt the city after each attack.

HUGO DE GROOT AND LOEVESTEIN

C HUGO DE GROOT (1583-1645)

PIONEER FOR MODERN INTERNATIONAL LAW

Hugo de Groot was a prodigy. At the age of 11, he studied at the University of Leiden. When he was 16, he was allowed to accompany the Grand Pensionary Johan van Oldenbarneveldt (1547-1619) to the King of France, in an attempt to get him to take the side of the Dutch in their fight against the Spanish. The French king called Hugo de Groot "the miracle of Holland."

De Groot, together with Van Oldenbarneveldt, was of the opinion that there should be room within religion for different ideas, and that the state stood be above the church. In 1619 Prince Maurits (1567-1625) took advantage of the religious disputes to arrest Van Oldenbarneveldt, with whom he often disagreed, and De Groot. Van Oldenbarneveldt was executed and De Groot was given a life sentence. He was locked up in Castle Loevestein.

De Groot was allowed to continue studying at Loevestein. With certain regularity, he would receive a chest filled with books. He escaped by hiding himself in a chest that was carried outside, and fled to Paris, where he lived on an allowance from the king.

In 1625, he wrote one of his most important works: *De iure belli ac pacis* (*On the Law of War and Peace*), which forms the basis of our current international law.

Hugo de Groot tried to return to Holland, but because he refused to submit an official request to the States of Holland or to the new prince, he spent the rest of his life in exile.

"This is Loevestein, a medieval castle. Here I kill three birds with one stone: Loevestein was, first of all, a castle; then it became the prison where Hugo de Groot was imprisoned; and finally it was rebuilt into a fort. This fort is something special because of the odd points where cannons were positioned to protect the surrounding land."

In 1361, Dirc Loef van Horne had a castle built on the borders of Gelderland, Brabant, and South Holland, which was an ideal location both for defense and for collecting toll.

In 1572, Willem of Orange had a fortification and a moat laid around the castle. Soldiers were barracked within the fortification walls. The castle itself became the State Prison for political and religious dissidents and prisoners of war. A century later, Loevestein became part of the Dutch Water Line.

In 1951, the military function of Loevestein was discontinued. The castle and the fortification are currently used as a museum and event location.

BEHIND THE DYKE

"Something I really can't believe is that houses are built directly behind the dyke. People cycle over the dyke, but the distance to the house is maybe only a yard. If you're a little tipsy, you could ride your bike straight into the people's front room. Not a very nice idea, if you ask me."

BETUWE LINE

"Here's the Betuwe Line. There was uproar about it in Holland. It is a very long railway line that runs right through the Betuwe. People were not in the least happy with that."

The Betuwe route was specially laid to transport goods from the Maasvlakte near Rotterdam to Germany.

From the very start there was a lot of protest, both from those living nearby and from the environmental movement. In the end, the construction cost more than twice the amount budgeted (€ 4.7 billion). The German link was not extended and less than half of the projected goods trains use the track.

KAREL DE GROTE

C CHARLEMAGNE (c. 742/748-814)

EMPEROR OF THE OCCIDENT

In 771, Charlemagne became ruler over the kingdom of the Franks, of which the later Holland would be a part. He was the most powerful monarch in the early Middle Ages and constantly expanded his empire. The Saxons and the Frisians were able to withstand the attacks of the Franks for a long time and thus preserve their independence. The Frisians supported the Saxons, who formed a buffer between themselves and the Frank kingdom. In 785, they were forced to give up their resistance and Magna Frisia also became part of the empire of Charlemagne who imposed Christianity on his subjects.

In 793, the Frisians rebelled one last time when Charlemagne forced the Frisians to fight with him against the Avars, a Turkish people. They started *en masse* to practice their old religion and persecute Christians but the rebellion was put down bloodily and ruthlessly.

Because Charlemagne was so immensely rich, he worked with liegemen to whom he gave authority over a certain region. In order to be able to consult regularly with them, Charlemagne had rich palaces everywhere, which were called *paltsen*. The Valkhof in Nijmegen was probably such a *palts*. Charlemagne would stay there for consultation with his liegemen and bishops from the region in order to follow the fight against the Saxons.

THE FORELANDS

"My other half requested, 'You won't forget the water forelands, will you?'

The forelands? What were they? They turned out to be the overflow areas for the rivers. There are both summer dykes and winter dykes along the rivers. The summer dyke is closer to the river, but in the winter the water sometimes rises so high that it streams over the summer dyke. The area behind—the overflow area—is submerged by the water. The winter dyke must then keep out the water."

Overflow areas arose in the middle ages. The summer dyke kept the water in check during the summer, so that the cattle grazing in the overflow area were protected. The flooding of the overflow area in the winter made sure that the land remained fertile.

ARCHITECTURE

"There are locks between the Biesbosch and the rivers. In the beginning, I didn't understand anything about the difference in water level everywhere in Holland.

You sail your boat up to such a lock and stop in front of the closed doors. You let the lock fill up with water until the level is the same as that on your side. Then the doors open and you sail into the lock. The doors close behind you. The doors at the other end are then opened just a bit to allow the water in the lock to sink to the level on the other side. You go down in your boat. Then the doors open fully and you can sail away. When you come from the other direction, everything happens in reverse. What I didn't know is that apparently a lot of argument takes place in the locks. It's a pity I didn't know that earlier. Now I've painted a lock that's much too small to show all that."

A lock as described above is known as a "pound lock." The Chinese engineer Chiao-Wei-yo developed the design in the tenth century. The first pound lock in Europe was constructed in 1373 in Vreeswijk, between the River Lek and a canal that led to Utrecht—a necessary connection for shipping.

"Vuren Fort is opposite Loevestein. That's also something special. It was originally intended for keeping an eye on the enemy, but it has never really functioned. They are now returning it to its original state."

Vuren Fort was built in 1844 as part of the New Dutch Water Line (see p. 36), but it has never been used as such. In the Second World War, the Germans occupied it, and after the war, it was used to imprison Dutchmen who had collaborated with the Germans during the war. Today, you can stay there in a Bed & Breakfast.

"This is the Martinus Nijhoff Bridge, named after the poet Martinus Nijhoff, because he always looked at the old bridge."
"I went to Bommel to see the bridge. I saw the new bridge." This is the start of the poem "The mother the woman" by poet and author Martinus Nijhoff (1894-1953).

The bridge Nijhoff wrote about was the Waal Bridge near Zaltbommel, built in 1933. It was replaced in 1996 and the new bridge—1080 yards long—was named after the poet.

"This is a lovely spot. That little island near Asperen only has one house on it, yet it is connected to the mainland by two bridges and a through road."

"At the top in the corner, I just about managed to save Kinderdijk. I really didn't know how to solve it, because it didn't fit anywhere, but I had a piece over here with nothing but green. That was perfect, because Alblasserwaard is also in this area, and that's where the row of windmills is."

The windmills of Kinderdijk (Children's Dike) pumped the water out of the Alblasserwaard peat area to make it a more habitable place. The first eight windmills of the Nederwaard water authority were built from stone and date from 1738. The eight windmills of the Overwaard water authority were constructed in 1740, have eight sides, are made of wood, and have thatched roofs. In addition, two octangular mills from 1740 and 1761 are in the Nieuw-Lekkerland polder, and there is a mill in the Blokweer polder, which is a reconstruction of a mill dating from 1620, which burnt down. The nineteen windmills together form Kinderdijk, the tourist attraction.

BRICK FACTORY

"In the distance, you can just see a brick factory that is also something characteristic for Holland. Because it is difficult to build on a sandy underground, almost everything is built with bricks. They make them themselves, which is why I've added this factory."

In the 12th century, monks made the first bricks in Holland; they used them to build their monasteries. Later the production of bricks for residential houses began, when more and more cities prohibited the construction of wooden houses because of the danger of fire they caused. Brick factories would often be located in the vicinity of the overflow areas, because there they could dig for clay for the bricks. In the 19th century, the number of brick factories grew explosively, but in the 20th century the number quickly declined. Today there are fewer than forty brick factories in Holland.

FIGURES FROM CHILDREN'S LITERATURE

C ANNIE M.G. SCHMIDT (1911-1995)
AGAINST THE PRIM AND PROPER DUTCH

Annie was the daughter of a vicar and liked writing verses, even at a young age. After working for some time as a librarian, she joined the newspaper *Het Parool* after the Second World War. There, she got to know the illustrator Fiep Westendorp (1916-2004) with whom she would make children's books throughout her life. Their first stories about Bob and Jilly appeared in the newspaper between 1952 and 1957.

At *Het Parool* she joined the cabaret group *De Inktvis* (*The Squib*), for which she also wrote lyrics and dialog. Annie wrote under the name Annie "M.G." Schmidt because there was already an Annie Schmidt who published books.

During her life she wrote radio and theatre plays, cabaret lyrics, verses for adults and children, essays and children's books. She also wrote the first Dutch musical, *Heerlijk duurt het langst* (*Delicious Lasts Longest*), for which Harry Bannink—with whom she worked for a long time—composed the music. In 1968, the incredibly popular *Ja zuster, nee zuster* (*Yes Nurse, No Nurse*) appeared on television,

again written by Schmidt with music by Bannink.

The work of Annie M.G. Schmidt is characterized by (for the time) strong language, which rebelled against the norm. Her stories for children were not sweet or pedantic, like many children's books at that time. Annie M.G. Schmidt said of herself that she had always remained "real."

"In May they have Annie M.G. Schmidt day. This parade is especially for Annie M.G. Schmidt and her illustrators."

This is Nurse Klivia from the television series *Ja zuster, nee zuster* broadcast in 1968. In the series, Hetty Blok (1920-2012) played Nurse Klivia. In the film made later, Loes Luca (1953) took over the role and in the musical version, the legendary character was played by Annick Boer (1971).

The first book of verse about the sheep Veronica and the sisters Groen appeared in 1951 under the title *Het schaap Veronica* (*Veronica Sheep*), illustrated by Wim Bijmoer (1914-2000).

Otje appeared in 1980 as a book, after first being published in *Margriet* as a serial. It was illustrated by Fiep Westendorp.

Sebastian the spider plays the main part in one of the famous verses by Annie M.G. Schmidt (*'This is the spider Sebastian. It didn't turn out well for him. LISTEN!*). The rhyme was published in the collection *Dit is de spin Sebastiaan* (*This is the Spider Sebastiaan*), with drawings by Wim Bijmoer.

"Abeltje, drawn by our master Thé Tjong-Khing."

The two books about Abeltje appeared in 1953 (*Abeltje*) and 1955 (*The A of Abeltje*) and were illustrated by Wim Bijmoer. Since 1980, Thé Tjong-Khing (1933) has drawn the liftboy.

"Bob and Jilly are on a board. They may only be illustrated two-dimensionally."

Between 1953 and 1960, eight books were published with stories about Bob and Jilly (Dutch: Jip and Janneke). Between 1963 and 1965, the stories were reissued into five volumes. Since 1977, the *Bob and Jilly Big Book* has been available with color illustrations in addition to those in black and white.

Annie M.G. Schmidt thought up the girl Dusty and her dog Smudge, who always managed to make himself dirty, for Persil detergent. Six books appeared, illustrated

by Fiep Westendorp, which were given away with the detergent. In 1973, the stories were collected and published as a book.

Pluk and his red tow-truck have driven out of the popular children's book *Tow-Truck Pluk*, which appeared in 1971 after first being published as a serial in *Margriet*. The book has been adapted into a radio play, musical, film, and Nintendo game.

FLIPJE

Flipje was born from a bewitched raspberry. He was thought up in 1935 by an advertising agency for the jam factory in Tiel, called De Betuwe. From 1936, the jam from De Betuwe was sold with the strip *Flipje, het fruitbaasje van Tiel*, (*Flipje, the Fruit Boss from Tiel*) drawn by Eelco ten Harmsen van der Beek (1897-1953). The "real" Flipje appears at all sorts of events. Tiel houses the Flipje and Regional Museum Tiel, with a wide selection of articles that have something to do with Flipje.

NIJMEGEN

"'Nijmegen is the oldest city in Holland, you'll be doing something with that, won't you?' asked my Nijmegen friends. No—I simply didn't have any room for it. That is why I made a panel especially for them advertising Nijmegen and the Four Days March that is always held there."

Even in prehistoric times, farmers inhabited the area near Nijmegen. Around the start of the Christian era, the place became a base of operations for the Romans. In the

year 71 AD, they founded Ulpia Noviomagus Batavorum, the largest town in the Low Countries. Nijmegen was granted city rights in 1230.

In 1678 and 1679, a series of peace treaties called the Peace of Nijmegen were signed in Nijmegen between Holland, France, Spain, and Sweden. This brought the end to the Dutch War (1672-1679).

In 1923, the Catholic University, later renamed the Radboud University, was opened in Nijmegen. In 1940, the city was the first in Holland to fall into German hands, and in 1944, bombing destroyed a large part of the city center. The city was completely rebuilt and has grown into a modern city that is, by population, the tenth largest city in Holland today.

The Nijmegen Four Days March—officially the International Four Days Marches in Nijmegen—traditionally starts on the third Tuesday in July. On four consecutive days, the participants march a distance of 30, 40 or 50 kilometers (18.1 24.1 or 31.1 miles). Everybody who completes the march receives the Cross for Proven March Skills, or the Four Days March Cross.

The event began in 1909 as a march for soldiers. Today, people from seventy different countries take part. During the Four Days March, soldiers will march either 40 kilometers with full backpack or 50 kilometers without backpack. Soldiers may wear the Four Days March Cross on their uniform.

NURSERY RHYME

White swans, black swans!
Who will come and sail to Angel Land?
Angel Land is closed
The key is broken
Isn't there any carpenter
who can mend the key?
Let's go
Let's go
Whoever's behind should take the lead!

This nursery rhyme probably originated in Teutonic times. Angel Land was the land of the angels, where the souls who did not have an earthly body lived. This Angel Land could only be entered using a key of bone.

"This illustration shows both the National Windmill Day and the National Bicycle Day. There are a lot of both bikes and windmills in Holland.
We are in North Holland, near the West Friesland Enclosure Dyke. What's so nice about this very old dyke is that whenever there was a flood, the people would leave the water where it was and just build the dyke with a bend around it. All the Dutch have a bike. That doesn't mean that there is a single type of bike. No, there are normal bikes, electric bikes, recumbent bikes, delivery bikes, mommy bikes, tandems, cross-country bikes, bikes with a low crossbar for the elderly, and so on. Sometimes there are seats for carrying a child or baskets for putting things in. There are some with windscreens, and with suspension systems for briefcases, hockey sticks, buggies, and strollers. If it's raining, you see some cyclists holding an umbrella, with the groceries hanging on the handlebars, children sitting on the back and a small kid just managing to cycle along beside, and yet it all turns out okay."

WINDMILL DAY AND BICYCLE DAY
SECOND HALF OF MAY

BICYCLES

"Some boys cycle with their hands behind their heads. That's cool."

"Carrier bikes were thought up for carrying children. But all at once, I was standing at the window talking on the phone when suddenly a man cycled by with such a bike, and in the carrier sat an old granny. I had to put that in and that gave me something amusing in this illustration."

"In the weekend, groups of friends jump on the bike to take a tour through the country. They race along dykes and cycle paths, disregarding everything. Often they put on the same shorts and shirts, so they look like a real pack. Young racers also take part."

The Bicyclists Association has been looking after the interests of 13.5 million cyclists since 1975. The association takes action for better road safety for cyclists and for fast bike routes. They try to tackle bicycle theft and improve the parking accommodation for bikes. Cyclists who become a member can make use of special discounts and advantageous offers and receive the membership magazine *De Vrije Fietser* (The Free Cyclist). The Bicyclists Association has 35,000 members.

"The Dutch will happily ride their bike with a baby in front of them and a second child on the back. Those children always fall asleep during the trip.
Naturally the older children have their own bike. Today, they have to wear a helmet."

"What I also like to see is a young boy cycling to his judo lesson already dressed in his judogi."

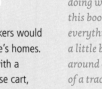

In the 19th century, bakers would deliver bread to people's homes. At first they did that with a pushcart, a dog or horse cart, then later with the traditional baker's bike.

"Once I sat in the train looking out—something I was always doing when I was working on this book because I wanted to let everything sink in—when I saw a little boy in a farmyard riding around on a tricycle in the shape of a tractor complete with a tiny manure tank behind it. That was for me!"

"There are also people who don't have children but dogs instead. They put those in baskets at the front and back."

"Hockey girls often hold their sticks as they ride their bikes."

HANSJE BRINKER

"This little guy is called Hansje Brinker. He put his finger in the dyke when he saw a hole in it, and in that way prevented

the dyke from collapsing. He is now part of Dutch culture, even though it seems that his story is not Dutch at all."
The book *Hans Brinker or The silver Skates* published in 1865 and written by the American author Mary Mapes Dodge (1831-1905) contains a story about the Hero of Haarlem: a young boy who sat with his finger in a hole in the dyke for a whole night. The little boy doesn't have a name, but when the story began to live a life of its own, he began to be called "Hans Brinker" after the main character in the book. Holland has adopted Hansje Brinker as a symbol of its struggle against the water. You can find statues of him in various places.

ESCAPED

"One day, I found an envelope from a friend of mine in my letterbox, with an article about a giraffe that escaped from Belly Circus in 2009. He just strolled quietly along the street, doing nobody any harm. Giraffes are very nice animals."
The giraffe of Belly Wien circus often escaped. In 2010, the animal was also found walking down a street in a Dutch village. For the political Party for the Animals it was reason to ask questions in the parliament to the Minister of Agriculture, Nature and Food Quality.

WINDMILLS

"For the windmills I first thought, 'I'll make one windmill, that'll be enough. After all, a windmill's nothing more than a thing with four sails.' But I should have known better. Just like bridges and bikes in Holland, there are different types of windmills, and they each do a different job. You've got tower mills, round towers, post mills; there are windmills for grinding corn, making paint, pumping water,

and then you've got smock mills, hollow post mills, etc. There's a lot more than you think.
It simply wasn't possible to illustrate all those types in scale. So I painted one at its proper size. That is the Zandhaas, a tower mill near us, in Santport. I could copy it, and nobody could then say it was wrong.
Because it is Windmill Day, there's a sign next to the road showing all sorts of windmills. Then, if you're interested, you can get off your bike and study them."

A **stage mill** is a windmill that is so high that there has to be a gallery where the sails can be adjusted to the direction the wind is blowing. Often a stage mill is between other buildings: the sails must then be high enough to catch the wind.

Stage mills are used to grid corn (corn mills), to press oil from seeds (oil mill) or to remove the husks from seeds (hulling mill).

A **round stage** is a stage mill in a round building.

"The post mill stands on legs and has a wooden stairway at the back by which to enter the windmill. These steps are fixed to a sort of turning circle, which means it revolves along with the mill. Wonderful."

The **post mill** is the oldest wooden windmill in Holland. It has existed since 1180.

This is a **paint mill**, which is a tower mill with a barn next to it where materials can be stored and dried. A paint mill often had various other grinding systems in addition to the one for paint wood, which could be used to grind the various color pigments so that the colors did not get mixed together. The first paint mill was taken into use in 1601 in Zaandam.

In a **paper mill**, paper is made from textile. Since a lot of water is needed when making white paper, nearly all paper mills are water mills and are driven by a wheel that is driven by streaming water. The last paper mill that runs on wind power is in Westzaan: De Schoolmeester (The Schoolmaster) from 1692.

A **tower mill** is a round stone windmill that grinds grain ground. The earliest known tower mill was built in 1280.

An **upper winder** is a mill where the cap of the mill to which the sails are attached can be rotated. There are three types of upper winder: the outside winder, where the cap is turned from the outside generally with a starting beam running down the back of the cap; the inside winder, where the cap can be turned from inside the mill using a special wind gear and wind rope; and the auto winder, which turns itself using a special system that reacts to the wind direction.

An **inside winder** is a upper winder where the cap can be turned from the inside.

A **belt mill** is both a stage mill and a ground sheeter (a mill where the sails can be operated from the ground). It is a windmill that stands on a hill, which is known as a "belt" in old Dutch. The "belt" contains poles for turning the sails into the wind. This type of windmill is mainly found in East and South Holland. In Limburg and North Brabant, they also talk of "mountain mill."

A **drainage mill** is also called a "water mill." The mill pumps water from lower land to higher land. It is a mill in which the miller makes not profit, because it does not produce anything. The water authority will pay the miller instead. The model illustrated is a wooden, eight-sided drainage mill where the cap can be rotated.

A **hollow post mill** is the oldest type of drainage mill in Holland. The first was built in 1407. The top part of the mill can be rotated completed above the pyramid-shaped under tower.

The **sawmill** is used to saw timber and consists of a stage mill constructed on a saw barn. It was Cornelis Corneliszoon (c. 1550-c. 1607) who fitted a crankshaft in a windmill and was able to transform the rotating motion into an up-and-down motion. He was awarded the patent on the sawmill in 1593.

"The tjasker is a very small mill. This one is in a field and you can even change its direction. As the streams in the field rise, it helps to dispose of the excess water."

The **tjasker** drainage mill is one of the smallest types of windmill. The tjasker was developed in Friesland.

"In addition to the windmills of the past, there is also the modern windmill that generates energy."

Windmills that generate electricity are called **wind turbines**. In the 1980s, they were only 16 yards tall, but after that they grew ever taller. By the middle of the 1990s they were 55 yards tall, and at the turn of the century, they had already reached nearly 110 yards high. It is projected that the ideal height will be somewhere between 160 and 210 yards.

Most turbines have three sails. Thanks to the distribution of the weight, there is the least possible stress on the axle, and on the bearing of the axle.

HISTORY

"The Dutch transport just about everything by water, even their cattle."

C COUNTRY HOUSES
(17th and 18th century)
WEALTHY LIVING OUTSIDE THE CITY

"The rich Amsterdammers left the city in the summer, because the canals stank so it was almost impossible to bear in the warm months. Those families didn't only take their staff with them, but also some of the furniture. The furniture was sent by boat and the family arrived in a coach. Gardens were laid out at the back of the country houses. The owners competed for the most beautiful garden. That's why I've exaggerated with this garden, which I thought was fun."

Most country houses were built in the 17th century, but even when the Dutch economy declined in the 18th century, the country house remained popular. Apparently the wealthy citizens didn't have much problem with the crisis.

Generally the women and their families spent the whole summer in the country and the men—who had to be in the city for their work—would occasionally join them.

Most country houses no longer belong to a family, but are tourist attractions or event locations.

C THE BEEMSTER (1612)
HOLLAND AND THE WATER

In 1607, a group of merchants and city councilors of Amsterdam decided to drain the Beemster in order to create agricultural land where food could be grown for the city's inhabitants.

A dyke was constructed around the lake and a belt canal was dug behind it. Windmill builder and hydraulic engineer Jan Adriaenszoon Leeghwater (1575-1650) was made responsible for fifty drainage windmills that pumped the water from the Beemster into the higher belt canal.

In 1612, the Beemster was dry. Use is still made of mills and pumps to keep the water in that area—which is divided into fifty sections—at the proper level. The water must be low in the agricultural areas, high in the residential area so that the piles under the houses do not rot away, and a level between the two for livestock farming. The hydraulic works are now completely automated.

AUCTIONS

"Auctions are even held on the water. The vegetable auction house was a very beautiful building where the growers could sail in with their boats filled with vegetables. I would have liked to put that in my book, but it didn't fit in."

The first vegetable "Dutch" auction was held at the Bakker Bridge in Broek op Langedijk in 1887. A Dutch auction is when the auction master starts at a high price and the price drops until somebody shouts "mine" and thus agrees to the sale. This type of auction is also called "descending price auction." The auction was first held in the open air. In 1912, a building was erected where the growers could sail their goods into the "bidding room." The building is now the Broeker Auction Museum.

TRADITIONS AND FESTIVALS

"The Dutch, as I mentioned earlier, love to show that there is a party somewhere. When a child is born, they hang a chain with 'Hooray a girl' or 'Hooray a boy' in the window. They run up the flag and hang up balloons. Sometimes a stork appears in the garden. Or, and they have them these days, they hang up a stork who seems to have got stuck while he was trying to fly in through the window."

The Dutch word for stork "Ooievaar" actually means "bringer of luck." The stork as a symbol of birth came to Holland in the 18th century from Germany. That is where the story began that the stork delivers the baby. The mother has to stay in bed

for a while because the stork has pricked her stomach with his beak.

Studies have shown that since the Second World War, the growth and decline in the number of storks in Holland runs parallel to the growth and decline in the number of births.

"The Dutch really love herring. In May, they have Flags Day in Scheveningen. I couldn't show that here, but I've included a bunch of flags as a reference to it."

The Dutch eat herring in a special way. The head is removed and they pick it up by the tail and let it slide in."

In the past, Flags Day—the Saturday before Whitsun—was the day on which the ships, decorated with flags, did a "test run" for the new herring season. The boats would then set out after Whitsun to fish for herring.

Today, Flags Day is when the first Dutch New Herring is brought on land. All the ships in the harbor are decorated and all sorts of events are organized.

The first barrel of New Herring is traditionally auctioned for charity. Every year, the Dutch eat 85 million New Herring.

"These are the cheese porters from Alkmaar and Gouda. The traditional cheese markets where the cheese is carried

around like this still exists. There's a knack to carrying cheese. I show two cheese sorts crossing each other."*

The cheese porters carry a wooden cradle between them on which eight large cheeses are placed. The weight of the whole thing is more than 130 kilograms. The porters walk in a certain way so that the cradle doesn't sway about too much—their walk is called the "cheese porters' shuffle."

The Alkmaar professional cheese porters formed a cheese porters' guild as long ago as 1622 that consists of thirty men and a cheese father. There are four groups of porters, with the colors red, yellow, green and blue. In the past, all cheeses on the cheese markets were carried on and off in this way, but today it has mainly become a tourist attraction. They also hold competitions.

DIVE

"If the weather's fine, you often hear screams and splashes as you cycle round North Holland. Children jump from the bridges into the water. That's not without danger, but they simply have to do it.

When we were cycling around to study everything, I saw a girl with a really nice bikini. There was a football on one breast, the other was orange and the bottom was orange with a black and white football belt. I simply couldn't draw it properly, because it would have been too small."

"Here is the rhyme, 'Sleep baby sleep.' This sheep has probably escaped through the rear of the farm building."

Sleep, baby, sleep
Outside there is a sheep
A sheep with white feet
That drinks some milk so sweet
Sleep, baby, sleep
Outside there is a sheep

FIGURE FROM CHILDREN'S LITERATURE

"This is a cow by Peter Spier, a great illustrator. The book about this cow is about what it's like in Holland. That's why he had to be included."

The American illustrator of Dutch origin Peter Spier (1927) made the picture book *The cow who fell in the canal* that first appeared in the United States in 1957 and a year later in Holland.

READING

"In the countryside or at large yards, you often see a trampoline.
This is the oldest son of the family where a child has just been born. He's thinking, 'Bah, a sister. I'm off to read a book.' He's lying on the trampoline with a book by Paul Biegel."

DUTCH SPECIALTIES

"I've also made some pigs, because there are a lot of those in Holland. I wanted to paint some happy pigs who were allowed outside."

Dutch pork has a good reputation internationally. Holland and Denmark are the leading producers of piglets. Each year, around 14.5 million pigs are slaughtered in Holland and 11.5 million are exported alive abroad.
In Holland, pork is the most eaten type of meat. The Dutch each 42 kilograms of pork per person per year. That is the average amount of meat you get from one pig.

"In Holland, chickens are often not allowed to run around outside, but these are. For here we have organic eggs."

On average, the Dutch eat 23 kilograms of chicken per person each year, the equivalent of 18.5 chickens.
The Dutch vocabulary has been enriched in recent decades with the word *plofkip* ("exploding chicken"). It refers to a chicken in the bio-industry that is reared in six weeks from a chicken

weighing 50 grams to a chicken weighing 2.2 kilograms. Today, more than 490 million *plofkips* are slaughtered each year, and the number continues to increase. Although organic products are becoming more accessible to the Dutch consumer, the market share is still under 3%. For organic meat, it is below 2%.

"In Dutch fields today, you not only find cows and sheep, but also, funnily enough, a sort of lama, the alpaca. They are bred for their wool."

What makes alpaca wool special is that it is hypoallergenic. Alpaca wool does not contain any fat, unlike sheep's wool. These South American animals were introduced into Europe in the early 1990s. Breeding in Holland only really got under way ten years later. The number of alpacas in Holland is growing rapidly.

"Ostriches—a little out of place in the Dutch countryside—are raised for their steaks."

Ostriches can be used for a lots of things: they lay eggs, their meat is in demand for consumption, their feathers and skin can be used for a whole variety of products, and their fat is used in cosmetics. In the 1990s, ostrich farms boomed in Holland, but the bird flu in 2003 left many of these companies bankrupt.
Many ostrich farms combine breeding with promotional activities and a shop featuring their own products.

"Here we see another boat with potatoes. The potato has also become Dutch."

The potato originally comes from South America. In the 16th century, it was taken to Spain by explorers. From there, monks spread it throughout Europe by planting potatoes in their monastery gardens. It was not until 1727 that the potato was recognized in Friesland as food, after which it began an unstoppable advance.

Today, the Dutch eat around 90 kilograms of potatoes each per year (including French fries, crisps and other potato products). One of the potato varieties bred by the Dutch is the *bintje*. It owes its name to Bintje Jansma (1888-1976), the brightest girl in the class of headmasters Kornelis Lieuwes de Vries (1854-1929) who bred potatoes in 1905.

Clogs are solid wooden shoes that are cut out of a block of poplar or willow. Since ancient times, laborers and farmers have walked around in clogs. Today you only ever see them in the country. Traditional clogs that are also on sale for tourists are painted yellow. In the past, every clog maker had a personal pattern so the painting showed who had made the clog.
During the week and at work, people would wear unpainted clogs. A man would wear black clogs to church and a woman wore clogs that were naturally varnished and decorated with a flower pattern.
Holland is often associated with clogs, tulips and windmills.

LAUNDRY

"On the farm, all the overalls are washed at the same time. They're hanging neatly next to each other on the line. The baby clothes are in front because you need a lot when you've just had a baby."

CANAL BOAT

"The canal boat is an unusual boat. Although it has a small sail, a horse that walks along the water or canal tugs it along."

SYMMETRY

"The Dutch like symmetry. If they place a vase on one side of the window, they want one on the opposite side as well. They also have, although you see it a lot less now than a few years ago, wooden ducks or geese in the window. If they want a change, they tie a ribbon around the creature's neck."

"We're in Groningen, with Lauwersmeer right at the top. I didn't want to show the city of Groningen, because we have enough cities in the book. The countryside is quiet and spacious; a nice contrast to those illustrations that are so full they make you dizzy. Of course, I couldn't stop myself making a reference to the city with its Martini Tower and the Groninger Museum, where they often mount really nice exhibitions. When we were driving around, I tried to imagine what was so different from the rest of Holland. A striking feature was all that space with enormous fields and gigantic farm buildings. There are people who cannot make a living from farming alone, and they open a campground on the farm, calling it 'Camping with the farmer.'
Apart for that, very little happens here. That's why I started a fire, then at least the fire brigade and the police will come into action. Don't worry; the fire will be all right. It's only included to liven things up."

GRONINGEN FIRST HALF OF JUNE

GAS

"They produce gas in Groningen. I've illustrated the NAM here with a grasshopper, an old pump that constantly goes up and down to extract gas."

☐ THE GAS BUBBLE (1959-2030?)
A FINITE TREASURE

In 1959, an enormous reserve of gas was discovered in the ground near Groningen. At the time, it was the second largest gas reserve in the world.

Thanks to this discovery, almost everybody in Holland switched to using natural gas instead of oil. A lot of gas is also piped abroad, but the gas production is not without problems. Because the gas is extracted from the ground, it can cause subsidence. This in turn can lead to earthquakes, and all the consequences those entail.

Producing gas is becoming increasingly difficult, because as the reserves decline, so does the pressure of the gas. The Nederlandse Aardolie Maatschappij (Dutch Oil Company) (NAM) would like to develop other fields, such as those in the protected nature area the Wadden Sea. Environmental groups are fiercely opposed to this.

Because gas production is of considerable economic importance for Holland—it contributes around ten billion euro per year to the treasury—and because the reserves are finite, choices will have to be made. What will be given precedence? Politics? Economy? Environment? The future will tell.

TRADITIONS

"People still get married in traditional costume. The labeled cows watch just like the little girl who looks round the corner of the house, 'What are my mother and father doing? Oh, they're getting married!'"

DOLPHINS

"They've got dolphins in the Dollard. Children really love dolphins, so this panel is for them."

The Dollard is a tributary of the Wadden Sea, which arose through flooding in the Middle Ages.
In them, at least thirty villages and three monasteries were "drowned." The river Eems flows into this tributary.
The brackish water tidal landscape is a rich natural area. Bird watchers can really enjoy themselves in various observation hides. There are also seals and the occasional porpoise. Porpoises are sometimes called "Dutch dolphins."

DUTCH SPECIALTIES

"The Dutch really love quality products. De Waard makes tents that can withstand gale force winds. Unbelievable. They're not tents, they're hotels made of fabric."

Machiel de Waard started a campsite in 1948. The summers were very wet and the campers quickly left their tents. That's why De Waard thought up the Albatross, a tent in which the ground sheet was sewn. It became a resounding success in rainy and windy Holland, and De Waard tents became a household word. New models were continuously developed, all known for their weather and wind resistance. De Waard is now the property of Vrijbuiter, but still exists as an independent brand. Around fifteen different models are available.

NURSERY RHYME

Farmer what do you say about my chickens?
Farmer what do you say about my cockerel?
Haven't they got beautiful feathers?
Or don't you like the color?
Farmer what do you say about my chickens?
Farmer what do you say about my cockerel?

FIGURE FROM CHILDREN'S LITERATURE

"Here stands Dik Trom. A few generations old, but everybody knows him."

Cornelis Johannes Kieviet (1858-1931) wrote five books about Dik Trom, the first in 1891. There was also a sixth book, but in that one, the son of Dik (who by then had grown into an adult) plays the main role. From the second reprint of the first book, the books were illustrated by Johan Braakensiek (1858-1940). There are several films about Dik Trom.

REGIONAL TRANSPORT

"This train is operated by a different company than those in the Randstad [the built-up area in the west of Holland]. There is only one track and the train goes back and forth."

Arriva Passenger Transport Holland operates the buses and trains in a number of regions in Holland. Arriva was formed in 1999 by merging a number of transportation companies.

Arriva trains run from the city of Groningen to places in the region, including Leeuwarden, Delfzijl, and Veendam.

"The distances are greater here and the train doesn't run every-

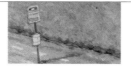

where. I think that's why there are so many bus stops. The signs often stand slightly crooked next to the road. They're not the usual yellow boards, but blue instead."

The blue bus stop signs indicate the city and regional transport of Arriva.

CAMPING

"What happens on a campsite? Father and mother put up the tent, but the last time they did it was a year ago, so they've forgotten exactly what to do. They get into an argument while their little boy holds up the flap at the back. But that's no problem, because he can quietly watch what's happening in the other tent."

"There are always families with two children—a boy and a girl—who tease each other a bit.

The girls can scream a bit harder than the boys so they get their pencils back and the boys get into trouble. The same happened in our house."

"These are my friends. Once a year, we go camping near our house in a De Waard tent, of course."

CROP CIRCLE

"Here is a crop circle. A colleague friend of mine knows all about them. I called her to tell her, 'Marianna, I've made a crop circle for you!'

'Which one?' she asked. Um, 'Which one did you have in mind?' I asked her. I ended up carefully copying it; apparently it has to be really precise."

ARCHITECTURE

"These are houses from the peat district. They actually stand on either side of the canal, but if I'd painted them like that, I would not have been able to include so many details.

I have chosen an intersection so that you have a good view. They are houses from the 1930s that are really worth looking at: small houses, designed with beautiful brick compositions. If you ask me, the bricklayers who worked on them really enjoyed themselves."

In the peat district, so-called ribbon villages stretch along the waterways where the peat is taken away.

"Farm buildings in Groningen have the living quarters at the front. The working quarters are behind them. You can recognize the living quarters from the beautiful windows, but it's odd that trees are in front of them,

which means the room is always in the shadow. This shows that on farms it's all about the work. The best room is for Sunday and not for any other time.

If the farm building is no longer in use as a farm, the trees are cut down and an elaborate garden is laid."

This type of farm building is sometimes called the "Oldambster farmhouse." The model came out of Germany to East Groningen at the start of the 18th century. The living quarters are narrower than the barn, and are connected to the barn with an extended ridge.

In the peat district there is a smaller version of the Oldambster farmhouse.

"What I never expected was to see this type of chic house along this road. It is a very unusual villa with a tower and balconies and a beautiful garden."

In Groningen, terps are called *wierde*. They are raised areas in the landscape that have been used since prehistoric times for building. Until dykes were built in the area around 1200, the terps provided protection against flooding.

"This is Den Andel, right at the very top of Groningen. This is where my accordion teacher lives, in the house belonging to the windmill."

The octagonal stage mill "De Jonge Hendrik" was built in 1875. It can grind grain and hull barley.

"This is an old tollhouse. They still exist, although nothing is paid any more. It is built in such a way that anybody sitting in it could see the horse and carts coming from some way in the distance. This house is in the Open Air Museum in Arnhem."

Originally this tollhouse stood in Bedum, since 1850. The toll collector maintained the road and in exchange for that charged a toll to those who made use of it. He lived with his family in the tollhouse. The custom of charging a toll disappeared in 1926 when the car tax was introduced.

"The old-fashioned electricity pylons are a bit like the Eiffel Tower. Straight light green pylons with small sidepieces are now gradually replacing the old pylons. The wires are also arranged above each other, so that the nuisance from radiation is a lot less."

The Martini Tower is more than 300 feet tall. It is nicknamed "d'Olle Grieze" (the old gray one) and belongs to the Martini Church. The tower was built between 1469 and 1482, after lightning destroyed two predecessors.

The current spire is from a later date—when the Spanish and Walloon left Groningen in 1577, bonfires were lit on the third battlement, which caused a fire and the top part collapsed up to a

height of 225 feet. The tower was also struck a number of times by lightning. In 1838, a lightning rod was mounted on it.

From the 18th century until 1921, the tower also served as watchtower and for fire duty.

Every Sunday and on special occasions, the Groningen Bell-ringers' Guild ring the twelve bells in the tower.

The Italian architect Alessandro Mendini (1931) was the chief architect for the striking building of the Groninger Museum that opened in 1994. The museum itself was founded in 1887. Other architects contributed to the museum with designs for pavilions (Michele de Lucchi [1951], Philippe Starck [1949] and the cooperative Coop Himmelb(l)au [founded in 1968]), a lounge (Studio Job, founded in 1997), an information center (Jaime Hayon [1974]) and a restaurant (Maarten Baas [1978]).

In addition to a rich program of exhibitions, in which all art movements are represented, the museum concentrates on North Dutch art by artists such as De Ploeg (an art collective founded in Groningen in 1918) and the expressionist Hendrik Werkman (1882-1945).

"The book is nearly finished so I wanted to end with a little peace and quiet. If it were up to me, I'd like to end up in the sea, in the same way as I began, but Holland isn't an island. That's why I've chosen the lakes in Friesland. In the middle of the book there's another one of those lakes, frozen over, with people skating on it. In the summer, the Dutch do all sorts of things on the water. I did some variation on the way the landscape looked. It's drizzling a bit here, but the Dutch don't mind."

SECOND HALF OF JUNE

THE FRISIAN LAKES

KIDS ON THE WATER

"Holiday time. Scouting is an important component in the life of many Dutch children. In the summer, you can even be a scout on the water."

The first scouting group in Holland was founded in 1910; at the time, it was called the "pathfinders." In sectarian Holland, various associations were founded from different life philosophies.

In 1941, when the pathfinders refused to merge with the National Youth Storm—the youth movement of the German-inspired National Socialist Movement—the German occupier prohibited their activities.

After the liberation, the associations were revived and in 1973 all the individual associations merged into one group now known as Scouting Holland.

There are ordinary scouts and water scouts. Between the ages of 10 and 16, children can become sea scouts. In addition to the usual scouting skills, these children also learn sailing and associated techniques.

"Despite the fact that Dutch children can swim well, they all wear a life jacket in a boat."

"This is a canal boat. If you didn't have a horse, but had children, the problem was solved. They had to pull the boat, on their own or with their mother because the skipper stayed on board. Today, they wouldn't allow something like that. In the Frisian Maritime Museum in Sneek, you can pull on such a rope to feel how heavy it was."

SKATING

"The Dutch skate in the winter. In the summer, those same people use in-line skates on land."

As long ago as 1700, a Dutchman invented wooden-wheeled skates for use in the summer. In 1760 came the model with iron wheels, which was improved over the years.

In 1979, the Dutch skate factory Zandstra invented the in-line skate, with five wheels. At the same time, the American brothers Scott (1960) and Brennan (1964) Olson invented the four-wheeled skate. Ultimately, the in-line skate proved the most suitable for long distances—comparable to a pair of *noren* racing ice skates—while the four-wheeled skate was preferable for shorter distances because of their maneuverability making them comparable to ice-hockey skates.

ARCHITECTURE

"Here, people live next the water. In reality, there is a whole row of these houses—the Dutch really like building rows of houses. It is built on piles over the water. Really nice, except that you don't have any land for a garden around it."

"There is a lot of space in the area above Sneek. There people build—and I'm not exaggerating—complete palaces. Here's the start of such a palace."

SOCCER

"I still had to show some children playing soccer. That's important."

FRYSK, FIERLJEPPEN EN SKÛTJESILEN

"People from Friesland have their own language, and you won't understand it unless you are Frisian. The place names are also translated. Sneek, for example, is called 'Snits' in Frisian."

In Holland, Frisian—*Frysk*—has the status of minority language. The language is recognized and protected in the *European Charter for Regional or Minority Languages*. In Friesland, Frisian is used in education, courts and tribunals, and in regional media. At secondary school, Frisian language and literature is an elective subject and it can also be studied at the University of Groningen. It is also possible to take Frisian as a minor subject at several foreign universities.

"In fierljeppen you use a pole to jump from one side of the water to the other. Great fun. Children do it, but it is also an official sport for grown-ups."
Poles used to be used to jump over ditches. It quickly developed into a game in which competitions were held. There are various associations for pole-jumping, or *fierljeppen* (Frisian) or *bongelwuppen* (Groningen dialect). Around one hundred official competitions are organized each year.

The Dutch Fierljep Bond organizes the annual Dutch Championships.

"Skûtsjes are old-fashioned boats, which were used in the past to transport just about anything. They are round, shallow, and have a brown sail. They are used for a sailing competition. This is a very big Dutch event."
The Frisian *skûtsjes* were built from the 18th century until c. 1930. The skipper would live with his family on board the steel or wooden *tjalk*. From the beginning of the 19th century, competitions were sailed with *skûtsjes*.
Since 1945, the Sintrale Kommisje Skûtsjesilen has organized the eleven-day competition that is held in the first two weeks of the annual construction sector vacation. In the third week of those vacations, the Iepen Fryske Kampioenskippen Skûtsjesilen has organized, since 1982, a championship over seven heats. Now that no freight is transported with the *skûtsjes*, the ships are often adapted to sail faster.

FIGURES FROM CHILDREN'S LITERATURE

"Ot and Sien. In the past, children learned to read with a primer in which Ot and Sien played the main role."
From 1902 onwards, Hindericus Scheepstra (1859-1913) and Jan Ligthart (1859-1916) wrote a whole series of

stories about Ot and Sien. Cornelis Jetses (1873-1955) made the illustrations for the very popular stories. In 1906, the four original sections with stories were published as *The Book of Ot and Sien*.

NURSERY RHYME

Under mother's umbrella
Walked two little kids
Hanneke and Janneke
They were best of friends
And the clogs went click-clack-click
And the rain went tick-tack-tick
On mother's umbrella
On mother's umbrella

PASSED!

When somebody hears that he or she has passed the exams in secondary school, they put out the flag together with a school satchel. It is a custom throughout Holland.

DUTCH SPECIALTIES

"In the museum in Sneek, we found out that KING peppermints are made in Sneek, in Friesland."
Candy factory Tonnema & Co. has, since it was opened in 1902, produced peppermints for various customers. In 1922, it launched its own brand known as Kwaliteit In Niets Geëvenaard KING (In Quality Equaled by Nothing). Chemist Paul van Hamel Roos (1850-1935) guaranteed the quality of the peppermint, which was promoted as "reviving and stimulating as a beneficial tonic." The portrait of Van Hamel Roos is still featured on every roll of KING.

"C&A began in Sneek. I had initially drawn it somewhere else completely, but a woman with two C&A bags is completely at home here."
In 1841, brothers Clemens (1818-1902) and August Brenninkmeijer (1819-1892) started a textile warehouse and a shop with ready-to-wear clothing. C&A (Clemens and August) was a success right from the very beginning. After they had conquered Holland, the family business expanded in 1911 into Germany and in 1922 into Great Britain. From the '60s, the company grew rapidly throughout the world. Today, C&A has around 1,500 branches in Europe and there are C&A's in Mexico, Argentina, Brazil and China. The Brenninkmeijer family is still owner of the holding company.

"Makkum ceramics are beautiful Frisian ceramics with flowers and the like."

The Tichelaar family has been making "consumer ceramics" in Makkum since c. 1640. The Royal Tichelaar Makkum works with yellow clay. After the first firing, a white covering tin glaze made in house is applied to the ceramics. Finely ground oxides are used for painting decoration on this underground. During the second firing, the colors appear.
There is Makkum white, with only the white tin glaze, Makkum blue, where a drawing in cobalt oxide is applied to the layer of white glaze, and Mukkum color, where the colors blue, yellow, green and red are used on white.

Joustra is a very common Frisian name. In addition to the Joustra Technical Services working on the construction of this house, there is another very famous Frisian Joustra who is also known as the Widow Joustra.
Widow Joustra was the wife of Hendrik Beerenburg, the inventor of Beerenburg, the traditional Frisian bitters. After the death of her husband, she started distilling the genuine Beerenburg in Sneek. The family business is still housed in the building where she began. Tours can be taken and drinks can be tasted. Today, there is a wide variety of liqueurs, fortified wines and jenever (Dutch gin).

MATA HARI

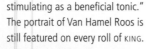

"An important figure in the history of Friesland is Mata Hari. She was an ordinary Frisian woman, nothing exotic, but she put on a nice little bra and an oriental dress, as if she came from a distant and mysterious country, and put herself forward as a spy."
Margaretha Geertruida Zelle (1876-1917) was born in Friesland and at the age of eighteen, married a captain of the Royal Dutch-East Indian army, who took her to Dutch East Indies. Two children were born there. Zelle learned the traditional dances and started calling herself "Mata Hari."
In 1902, the marriage fell apart. Mata Hari left for Paris where she worked as a horsewoman in a circus and as an artist's model. Later she started performing exotic striptease acts.
Rumors that she mixed in the highest circles and led a luxurious life quickly began. She had affairs with highly placed French soldiers. During the First World War, the French intercepted a message from the Germans, which stated that they had received valuable information from Mata Hari. Mata Hari was arrested. Even though she wrote to the Dutch consul that she was only a dancer, she was sentenced to death in 1917 for espionage and executed.
Her life has been a source of inspiration for countless films, books, plays, a Broadway musical, and a television series.

AKWADUKT

"This is the Princess Margriet Canal that crosses the freeway."
The Middle Friesland aqueduct —Akwadukt Mid-Fryslân—carries the Princess Margriet Canal over the A32 at Grou. It opened in 1993.

FLOATING GARDENS

"The Dutch even have gardens on the water. I have stolen these from Amsterdam."
Artist Robert Jasper Grootveld (1932-2009), who called himself a "visionary storyteller" and "building artist," developed the idea of *The Floating Gardens of Yuppopolis.* He constructed rafts of Styrofoam on which he planted gardens. The first three rafts were launched in 2000 near the Amsterdam city district of Zeeburg. People living near water have been making small floating constructions on which they get plants to grow for quite some time.

MUSEUM

"We went in whenever we came across a museum in our trip through Holland. I say 'we', because my other half accompanied me throughout the whole journey. He drove, I drew. In the Frisian Maritime Museum in Sneek, we saw a showcase with a small children's coach that was the coach of the orphans of Sneek. And you know what? My other half's grandmother spent time in that orphanage as a child."

The Old Orphanage of Sneek was founded in 1581. In the centuries following, the orphanage was housed in a variety of buildings. From 1870, it also accepted Catholic orphans. As the need for giving homes to orphans rapidly declined in the 20th century, no more orphans were admitted after 1931. In 1938, the orphanage closed its doors.
The wooden goat-cart was donated to the orphanage in 1923 by Leopold Hertzberger (1871-1933), when he resigned as regent.

FRISIAN HORSE

"This is a Frisian horse. Frisians are beautiful, big horses, with hair at the bottom of their legs."
The Frisian is the oldest Dutch thoroughbred horse. It is a strong, powerful horse with short, longhaired legs. The Romans were very taken with the quality of this strong creature and used it as a warhorse.
The horse is bred as a working horse that worked the land for six days a week and on Sunday would be harnessed to the coach to take its owner to church.

"All at once, I knew the Enclosure Dyke was exactly how to finish the book! I was so happy when I thought of it. At the bottom you see what used to be the Zuiderzee. That is now the IJsselmeer. On the other side is the sea. That wonderful dyke separates the two and brings the book to a close."

THE ENCLOSURE DYKE

CORNELIS LELY

"Cornelis Lely designed the Enclosure Dyke."

The politician Age Buma (1820-1893) tried for some time to garner support from the Lower Chamber and the Frisian States to drain the Zuiderzee. When that failed time and again, he gathered the support of countless influential private individuals and in 1886 founded the Zuiderzee Association, which had the aim of reclaiming the land. Hydraulic engineer Cornelis Lely (1854-1929) joined the Zuiderzee Association in the year it was founded. In 1887,

he was put in charge of the Technical Office. In 1891, he developed the plan for reclaiming the land that became the Zuiderzee Works.

It took until 1918 for the Zuiderzee Act, which stated that the Dutch State would finance an enclosure dyke, to pass. Even though Lely was himself the Minister of Water for many years, this did not hasten the decision-making process.

The construction of the Enclosure Dyke began in 1927. In 1932, it was completed. Lely did not live to see it.

DUTCH SPECIALTIES

"The Dutch like 'drop' also known as liquorice. A truckload of drop can never be too big."

Holland is the largest manufacturer of *drop* in Europe and earns an annual revenue of around one hundred million euro. The Dutch eat an average of two kilograms of drop per year (of the 11.5 kilograms of sweets they enjoy). *Drop* is candy you have to learn to eat. Most people, when they taste it the first time, think it's awful.

The most important ingredient of *drop* is liquorice root, which gives the product its black color. The salt taste is derived from salmiak—salty liquorice—and the rest of the sweet contains between 30 and 60% sugar. For the rest, the ingredients vary for each *drop* sort and there are hundreds of them. Important *drop* manufacturers are Red Band Venco, Klene and Katja.

THE MARINE DAYS AND FLORA AND FISHERY DAYS

The Marine Days, which used to be called the National Fleet Days, are held every year in July in Den Helder. They are intended as promotion for the Dutch Navy. Demonstrations on the water, on land, and in the air are intended to show the Royal Navy's readiness for battle.

Den Oever used to be on the island of Wieringen. In 1924, the island ceased to exist after the construction of the Amsteldiep Dyke, also known as the Short Enclosure Dyke. The real Enclosure Dyke begins at Den Oever. At the end of the summer, Den Oever hosts the annual Flora and Fishery Days that are a combination of a flower show and a fleet show with a wide range of events on land.

CYCLING

"And there are always the die hards who cycle across the Enclosure Dyke with a heavy backpack and preferably against the wind. It is nearly 19 miles, but they simply have to do it."

GERMANS

"Who comes to Holland a lot on vacation? Germans, because they don't have as much sea as the Dutch."

EEL

Along the Enclosure Dyke, there are the piles and the tops of the traps that show that they are fishing for eel in the IJsselmeer. The economic value of the Dutch eel branch is around 250 million euro per year.

Since 2011, no eel may be exported from the European Union, in order to allow the eel population to increase. In Holland, the Sustainable Eel Sector Holland Foundation (DUPAN) has been set up, and, among other things, it puts eel over the dyke. They catch the eels in front of the pumping stations in North Holland and Zeeland and release them in the sea, so that they can swim unhindered to their mating place.

FIGURES FROM CHILDREN'S LITERATURE

"Here are two mice by Thé Tjong-Khing; they have stolen the cake."
Where is the cake? by Thé Tjong-Khing (1933) appeared in 2004.

Miss C. Mouse and her dog Lucebert have been enjoying adventures in several books since 2007; the stories are written by Erik van Os (1963) & Elle van Lieshout (1963) and illustrated by Marije Tolman (1976).

NURSERY RHYME

All who want to sail as privateer
Must be men with beards
Jan, Piet, Joris and Corneel
They have beards, they have beards
Jan, Piet, Joris and Corneel
They have beards, they'll sail along

In the original version of this sea shanty, the names of the men with beards are Jan, Pier, Tjores and Corneel. Over the years, they have changed into names that were more usual at the time.
"Privateer" was a captain who was given permission by his country to attack ships of enemy countries—piracy with permission, you could say.